"If you want to be the best you can be and find practical ways of improving yourself then this book will take you through some easy-to-follow steps and ideas to make the most out of the opportunities you have."
Dame Sarah Storey, 11-times Paralympic Gold medallist

"*How To Win* is fun to read, strong on evidence and full of useful techniques – an ideal book for those wanting to get into 1st place."
Dr. Sebastian Bailey, Co-Founder and President, Mind Gym

"We all want to be winners in life, but to win ethically and well would be the ideal. As with his previous books, Rob's advice is practical, to the point and above all effective. Another must read – and must do!"
Julian Ranger, Founder and Chairman, SocialSafe

"This book is a winner in every respect. Evidence-based advice in a well-constructed, highly-readable and easily-recalled format. What's stopping you being a winner? Perhaps it's the fact you've yet to read Rob Yeung's excellent book."
Robert Kelsey, Author of What's Stopping You? *and* What's Stopping You Being More Confident?

"*How to Win* provides practical information to people on getting ahead in their career, the soft skills necessary to be successful at work, from networking to being more assertive to using political skills. This is a must-read for anyone wanting to succeed in their jobs and careers."
Professor Cary L. Cooper, CBE, Distinguished Professor of Organizational Psychology and Health at Lancaster University Management School

"Inspirational but with practical tips – a must-read whether you're starting out or an experienced professional."
Carol-Ann White, Global Human Resources Director, branding consultancy FITCH

"*How to Win* is a great blend of compassion and practical experience. Dr Rob Yeung provides simple and logical steps to making a difference and wraps each one in stories and examples that speak to everyone. This book will make you rethink your approach to every situation and applying the ideas will change your life and performance at work in a very positive way. Highly recommended."
Gary White, Chief Executive, sales technology company White Springs

"We would all like to win a bit more often and Dr Rob's book helps you do just that. The more you read this book, the greater the likelihood that you'll win."
Marc Woods, 12-times Paralympic medallist, winner of 21 medals from European and World Championships and bestselling author of Personal Best

How to Win

The Argument
The Pitch
The Job
The Race

Dr Rob Yeung

CAPSTONE
A Wiley Brand

© 2014 Dr Rob Yeung

Registered office
John Wiley and Sons Ltd, The Atrium, Southern Gate, Chichester, West Sussex, PO19 8SQ, United Kingdom

For details of our global editorial offices, for customer services and for information about how to apply for permission to reuse the copyright material in this book please see our website at www.wiley.com.

The right of the author to be identified as the author of this work has been asserted in accordance with the Copyright, Designs and Patents Act 1988.

Wiley publishes in a variety of print and electronic formats and by print-on-demand. Some material included with standard print versions of this book may not be included in e-books or in print-on-demand. If this book refers to media such as a CD or DVD that is not included in the version you purchased, you may download this material at http://booksupport.wiley.com. For more information about Wiley products, visit www.wiley.com.

Designations used by companies to distinguish their products are often claimed as trademarks. All brand names and product names used in this book and on its cover are trade names, service marks, trademarks or registered trademarks of their respective owners. The publisher and the book are not associated with any product or vendor mentioned in this book. None of the companies referenced within the book have endorsed the book.

Limit of Liability/Disclaimer of Warranty: While the publisher and author have used their best efforts in preparing this book, they make no representations or warranties with the respect to the accuracy or completeness of the contents of this book and specifically disclaim any implied warranties of merchantability or fitness for a particular purpose. It is sold on the understanding that the publisher is not engaged in rendering professional services and neither the publisher nor the author shall be liable for damages arising herefrom. If professional advice or other expert assistance is required, the services of a competent professional should be sought.

Library of Congress Cataloging-in-Publication Data is available

A catalogue record for this book is available from the British Library.

ISBN 978-0-857-08429-3 (paperback) ISBN 978-0-857-08427-9 (ebk)
ISBN 978-0-857-08426-2 (ebk)

Cover design by Parent Design Ltd

Set in 10/13 pt SabonLTStd by Toppan Best-set Premedia Limited
Printed in Great Britain by TJ International Ltd, Padstow, Cornwall, UK

To Steve Cuthbertson – I picked a winner that 20th July! To my parents – for loving me and supporting me so totally that I shall always feel like a winner. And to my board of directors Lou Stockden, Nichola Schwarz, Chie Miyadera, Lena Fedoruk, Chris Bailey and Dan Smith for keeping me chilled.

Contents

About the Author

Dr Rob Yeung is a highly regarded coach and the author of over 20 books, including bestseller *Confidence*. As a director at leadership consulting firm Talentspace, he helps organizations to identify highfliers; he also coaches and trains leaders and entrepreneurs to improve their performance.

Also an in-demand keynote speaker, he is known for giving entertaining yet insightful speeches at conferences worldwide. He is frequently asked to speak on topics such as the psychology of leadership, sales success, change and high achievement. In both his consulting and speaking work, he distinguishes himself by basing his recommendations on scientific research.

In addition, he provides regular expert commentary on television, including for both CNN and the BBC. He has written for the *Financial Times* and the *Guardian* and been quoted in publications ranging from *Men's Health* and *Glamour* to the *Wall Street Journal*.

www.robyeung.com

www.twitter.com/robyeung

Acknowledgements

Thanks first of all to Holly Bennion and the Capstone publishing team for persuading me to write for you guys – it's been a smooth and enjoyable process so far! Thanks also to my Talentspace colleagues for giving me the time and space to write in peace. And, of course, thank you to those of my coaching and corporate clients for putting your trust in me and allowing me to share some of your stories.

Introduction

The will to win, the desire to succeed, the urge to reach your full potential . . . these are the keys that will unlock the door to personal excellence.
Confucius

Do you want to be a winner? Yes, of course you do. Silly question really. Because, by definition, if you're not winning, you're losing. And no one wants to be a loser.

In sports, there's always a clear victor. Whether it's in a tennis tournament, a football match, a 100-metre race or something else in track and field, it's easy to spot the winner: it's the person or team that scored the most points, ran fastest, threw furthest, lifted more weight or whatever.

But how exactly do you win *in life*?

If you think about it, life is full of opportunities to win or lose on a daily basis. Every time we have a discussion, negotiation or disagreement with a colleague or boss, family member or friend, we could win by persuading them to do things our way.

Then there are the breaks that make the biggest differences in our lives – those inflection points such as job interviews that could take our lives in amazing directions if we win. They don't come along very often, but beat the other candidates to win the job and you may get greater responsibility, more exciting work and a bigger salary. It could present you with fresh opportunities and take your career to a whole new level. Lose and you end up with nothing.

Or think about those presentations we have to deliver occasionally. Sell your product or service to a client and you could land a big account with perhaps a juicy bonus for yourself. Present a novel concept successfully to investors and you could find yourself a mogul in the making. Appeal to a group of potential donors about the merits of your charity and you could find them lavishing funds on your cause.

This book is about winning the argument, the pitch, the job and – ultimately – the race. So, come with me if you would like to win.

Do you want to be a winner? Yes, of course you do.

The appliance of science

Before we move on, let me pose a question and try to answer it too: Why should you do what this author – this Rob Yeung guy – is telling you? After all, you may have read other books telling you to do things this way or that but maybe not got the results you wanted.

Allow me to answer the question by telling you a bit about me. I started my career as an academic. After graduating with an under-graduate degree in psychology, I worked for a year as a research assistant before embarking upon a three-year PhD in psychology at the Institute of Psychiatry, a five-star-rated research department and part of King's College London.

And what I primarily learnt in those seven years was the importance of *evidence* – of having scientific *proof* about what works and what doesn't.

Even though we may not think about it often, evidence matters in so many areas of our lives. Imagine if doctors prescribed drugs or recommended surgery on the *hunch* that it might help patients.

Without quantifiable evidence that their techniques worked, they could end up harming rather than healing. No, clearly we want doctors to treat patients using only medicines and techniques that have been trialled and *proven* to work.

Or consider how you would feel if a team of engineers said that they had designed and built a brand-new kind of aeroplane that should be able to get from London to New York using less fuel than ever before. The only snag is that they haven't done any tests. They wholeheartedly *believe* that it will work. However, they have *no proof* that it will be able to make the journey across the Atlantic without falling apart or bursting into flames. Would you get on that plane!?

Make no mistake: evidence has a crucial role to play in ensuring that the things we do are safe and genuinely valuable in our every-day lives. So why should this not be the case in the realm of self-improvement too? Surely if we aspired to lift our game and boost our performance – either in our professional *or* personal lives – we should follow only recommendations that were supported by proof, right?

The science of winning

I completed my doctorate in psychology over 15 years ago. Since then, I've been working as a psychology consultant to companies ranging from perhaps the world's favourite airline to high street banks such as HSBC, accountancy firms including KPMG and media organizations such as the BBC.

I train managers in how to become better leaders – in how to inspire and engage employees to work more productively. I coach entrepreneurs and salespeople on how to win over investors and clients. I run workshops and give speeches on topics ranging from how to identify talent in the workplace to becoming more charismatic and confident. And in all of my work, *I try as far as possible to recommend techniques and interventions that work (i.e. ones that are backed by scientific evidence)*.

The good news is that there is plenty of research into the science of career success and life satisfaction. There are professors at leading business schools – experts in marketing, economics, management and human communication – as well as psychologists and other scientists at top universities all over the world working tirelessly to figure out what helps certain individuals to get ahead.

My job is simple: I'm just presenting this stuff for you in one handy collection. If you want ways of getting ahead that are proven to work, this is the book for you.

As we move from chapter to chapter, I'll illustrate the various principles and techniques I recommend with case studies of folks I've met or worked with. In some cases, I've changed people's names and some personal information to protect their anonymity.

But hopefully these stories will allow you to see how the tools and tactics within this book may be able to help you too.

> If you want ways of getting ahead that are proven to work, this is the book for you.

Navigating through this book

I've laid out the book into five chapters and a conclusion, as follows:

- **Chapter 1: Developing a Winning Outlook.** A substantial body of research tells us that a critical factor that differentiates winners from losers isn't what you do – but how you *think* about yourself. So, before I get into how to win arguments or pitch ideas and so on, in this chapter I'll tell you how you can set yourself up with this winning perspective.

- **Chapter 2: Winning the Argument.** Psychologists know that most people aren't very good at getting their point across. Some individuals are too aggressive (which only makes others resent them), while many are too passive (which means they rarely get what they want). Thankfully, research tells us how to come across well: to be assertive, influential and persuasive while at the same time being respected and even liked. Want to know how? In this chapter, I'll present the tools and techniques that allow us to broach differences of opinion and get what we want.

- **Chapter 3: Winning the Pitch.** Pitching is the skill of influence, persuasion and selling *anything*. Of course, that's useful for selling actual products or services if you work in sales. More importantly though, pitching means being able to sell ideas and even ourselves – skills that we *all* need, no matter what we do for a living. Want to raise money for charity? You have to sell your cause. Want to get that promotion? You have to sell yourself. Want someone to go out on a date with you? Yes, even that is selling. But rather than trying to turn you into a pushy salesperson, I'll give you a scientifically proven weapon for influencing, persuading and pitching just about anything: storytelling.

- **Chapter 4: Winning the Job.** Job interviews are arguably the most significant inflection points in our careers. Get the right job and all sorts of opportunities could open up. But rather than tell you stuff you already know, I'll cover some counterintuitive but useful findings based on the science of job hunting. For instance, what does psychology say about lying during interviews and our chances of getting caught out? What eight interview questions have psychologists discovered you *must* know the answers to? And, if there's *one* thing you could do to improve your chances of finding a brilliant new job, what would it be? I'll reveal the answers to these questions – and more – in this chapter.

■ **Chapter 5: Winning the Race.** Ever wondered what the secret, unspoken rules of success at work are? This chapter has some answers as researchers now know a surprising amount about the skills and behaviours that allow certain individuals to leap forwards in their careers while others languish behind. I'll talk about the importance of doing all of the stuff that *isn't* mentioned in your job description. I shall explain the ways in which managing your working relationships leads to better prospects and promotions. I'll also cover how modern careers require a novel kind of thinking about developing the *right* skills – and how you can find a niche that will propel you up the career ladder.

■ **Conclusions: Onwards, Upwards and Over to You.** This book is packed, packed, packed with content and it would be easy to take on too much or feel overwhelmed by everything that you *could* be doing. Rather than leaving you to struggle with putting the principles into practice, I'll finish the book with easy-to-follow guidelines on how to set effective goals and keep your motivation high. All you need to do is put in the work and your success is pretty much guaranteed.

> **Over to you**
>
> I hope that this is a book you can *apply* rather than a book that you will simply read and then set aside. So throughout the book, I shall include boxes like this one to spell out how you could put certain principles or manoeuvres into practice to benefit not only your professional but perhaps also your personal life.

There are lots of books out there on how to get ahead in life. But I truly believe that this book is unique because the tools and techniques within it have been *proven to work*. Based on scientific evidence, we know that certain skill sets and mind-sets help people to succeed.

But this isn't a dry, technical manual about how to win in life. As well as being educational, I guarantee that the book will be entertaining too. Along the way, we shall discover how thinking about pies and baking can help us to become better negotiators. We'll learn what Harry Potter, Luke Skywalker and Jesus Christ all have in common. And we'll see how asking for a ridiculously massive salary can genuinely help you to extract more money from your boss.

This book is unique because the tools and techniques within it have been proven to work.

Ready to get started? Let's begin in Chapter 1 by investigating how our beliefs can either trap us or empower us to change. Because it so happens that just a single sentence may be all it takes to alter your ability to achieve.

1

Developing a Winning Outlook

Leaders are made, they are not born. They are made by hard effort, which is the price which all of us must pay to achieve any goal that is worthwhile.
Vince Lombardi

This chapter is all about attitude. So let's kick off by exploring your views about yourself. Of course, I'll explain everything shortly.

Below are a set of rating scales for different qualities and characteristics. Take a couple of moments to weigh the extent you believe each one is either an innate talent or something that can be developed, taught and honed.

For example, if you think that intelligence comes down entirely to a natural endowment – to the gifts that you are born with – then you'd give it a score of 1 out of 10. If you believe that intelligence is 100 per cent determined by hard work and effort, then you'd give it a score of 10 out of 10. Or if you consider that it's 50/50, then you'd give it a score of 5.

Want to give it a try?

Intelligence:

1 _____ 10

Natural talent   *Skill you can develop*

Creativity:

1 _____ 10
Natural talent   *Skill you can develop*

Leadership:

1 _____ 10
Natural talent   *Skill you can develop*

The ability to tell jokes and make people laugh:

1 _____ 10
Natural talent   *Skill you can develop*

Charisma:

1 _____ 10
Natural talent   *Skill you can develop*

Athletic ability:

1 _____ 10
Natural talent   *Skill you can develop*

Public speaking:

1 _____ 10
Natural talent   *Skill you can develop*

Patience:

1 _____ 10
Natural talent   *Skill you can develop*

For as long as I can remember, I've been curious about human behaviour and what drives people. But training to become a psychologist has taken that inquisitiveness about folks to a whole new level. And now as a psychologist working mainly with businesses, it's my job to be able to size people up – to evaluate them and come to judgements about not only how good they are but also how far they'll progress in their careers.

One of the biggest differentiators between winners and runners-up in life is their attitude. Over the years, I've learnt that one of the biggest differentiators between winners and runners-up in life is their attitude. But to illustrate exactly how outlook can matter, let me tell you about a pair of managers I first met more than a half-decade ago, whom I'll call Anna and Matthew.

It's all in the mind

Organizations often ask me to rate the strengths and weaknesses of their managers. I've been working with one particular company, an international insurance company for quite some time now. The top bosses asked me to audit 45 of their most senior executives in the UK on a four-point scale of their potential. A "1" meant that the executive was a star with plenty of potential to take on bigger roles not just within the UK but also internationally; unfortunately, a "4" meant that the executive had probably been over-promoted and should be shuffled sideways into a less demanding role.

The assessment process began with all of the executives, including Anna and Matthew, filling out surveys asking them to rate their own strengths and failings across assorted categories of capabilities, such as "Inspiring people" and "Making business decisions". Next, at least six colleagues also filled out similar surveys to rate each executive. Finally, I met with each executive individually to discuss their scores, interview them about their leadership successes and failures, and ultimately decide what rating – on that four-point scale – I would give them in terms of their continuing potential.

I spent two hours with each executive. Matthew stood out for his confidence, charisma and unerring certainty about himself. A lanky figure with a broad smile and a crushing handshake, he was clearly someone who was used to making headlines. He received mainly complimentary comments from his colleagues, who said that he was a strong leader that they could turn to for guidance when they weren't sure what to do.

Sure, he had a few shortcomings, but didn't everyone? I told him about some of the occasional discrepancies between how he rated himself and how his colleagues rated him. For example, they said that he could at times be absolutely certain he was right even when he was later proved to have been wrong. He also tended not to revise his opinions easily.

In response, Matthew shrugged his shoulders and agreed that no one was perfect. He smiled and said, "Well, I've always been like that – it's a bit too late to change now!" The implication: as a manager in his late 40s, he was simply too old and too set in his ways to change.

Anna was much less sure of herself. A slender woman who moved with the energy of a skittish doe, she had reached the same executive grade as Matthew and was perhaps a couple of years younger than him. However, she admitted privately that she still had so much to learn about how to lead her team effectively.

She received a mixture of comments from her colleagues and clearly wasn't happy with everything she heard. They admired a lot about her analytical mind and empathy but said that she could demonstrate more energy and enthusiasm in front of her team. They felt that she was sometimes reluctant to take decisions in the face of uncertainty too.

Anna puffed out her cheeks with disappointment at a few of the comments but listened and made careful notes. She asked sensible questions to understand the less flattering remarks that colleagues had made about her perceived failings.

She was eager for my input too. Whereas Matthew had demonstrated much greater certainty in his own ability to progress in his career, Anna sought much more guidance from me. She asked questions such as "In your experience, how have other managers addressed such issues?" and "What could I do to make the biggest difference to my leadership skills?"

So who would you think had the greater potential? Matthew or Anna?

Gifts versus growth

I first met Matthew and Anna nearly six years ago. And as I've continued working with the insurance company, I've seen how the two have progressed. Eighteen months after I first met him, Matthew was promoted into an even more senior role, looking after all of the human resources managers within the UK business. It was what Matthew and everyone else around him had expected. He was a formidable performer within the business and to this day remains a solid, dependable executive with a lot to contribute.

But what about Anna, who felt she still had so far to go?

She got promoted twice and now looks after all of the people – not just the sales team but also the finance managers, technology experts, human resources folk and so on – across all of northern

Europe, including the UK. She skipped a grade ahead of Matthew and is now his boss too.

But when I met her only a few months ago, she said that she still doesn't have all the answers. She maintains that she has a great deal to learn. She believes that the world is changing so swiftly and she can only just keep up.

And so we come to the crux of the tale. An increasingly convincing tidal wave of research shows that one of the biggest predictors of how well we do in not just our careers but our lives in general is down to our attitude, our outlook on life.

Matthew has an example of what I call a "gifts mind-set".[1][*] He believes himself to have certain gifts or talents but also certain weak spots that he doesn't think he can change. His strengths are that he is confident, charismatic and decisive. At the same time, he accepts that he has flaws: he can be more certain of himself than situations sometimes warrant. And he doesn't always listen to what others have to say – he doesn't change his mind often.

He sees his strengths as well as his weaknesses as aptitudes that have been bestowed upon him – as traits that are pretty much fixed and difficult to modify. You might as well ask him to alter his eye colour or height. Take him or leave him. That's the way he is now.

Anna, on the other hand, possesses what's known as a "growth mind-set". She tackles every new situation with the attitude that it's an opportunity for her to learn. In my very first meeting with her,

---

[*] Most readers can enjoy the book without turning to the notes at all. Notes are provided principally for more academically minded readers who may wish to read the original scientific papers.

she was almost greedy to learn all she could and find out how she could improve. Far from feeling confident about her abilities, she was almost painfully aware of how much more she could learn.

She felt that everything was amenable to change – her strengths as well as her failings. She saw herself as a work in progress rather than a finished product. Even today, she continues to feel that she has much to learn – that she is *still* a work in progress.

Of course, you may be thinking that other factors have determined Anna's and Matthew's careers. Perhaps Anna got lucky. Maybe Matthew had personal problems that distracted him. But actually, there is a huge body of scientific evidence confirming that our belief in our own capacity to change matters so, so much.

Here's the science bit

People with the gifts mind-set believe that their traits and psychological characteristics are fixed. Broadly speaking, people with the gifts mind-set believe that their traits and psychological characteristics are fixed. Such individuals feel that their intelligence, creativity, empathy, ability to learn new languages and so on are gifts that they only have a certain amount of. What you get when you're born is all you get – and that's the end of the story. Whether you're good, great or below average at something is due to the endowments that were passed on to you. And when you falter at a task, it's down to an absence of that ability.

In contrast, those with the growth mind-set believe that their traits are much more malleable and amenable to change. They feel that, yes, even their most fundamental qualities such as their very creativity, or even morality, can be improved through education and effort. As a consequence, they look at failure as demonstrating not an insufficient ability but a lack of exposure, opportunity or hard work.

So what? How do these different ways of thinking help us?

Those with the growth mind-set believe that their traits are much more malleable and amenable to change.

It turns out that growth-oriented people tend to do better in all sorts of situations. They tend to tackle new challenges with relish because they believe that they will learn more from taking on fresh challenges than from sticking to tasks and issues that they're familiar with. They tend to stick with difficult problems for longer. They also bounce back from failures more swiftly as they see mistakes as a necessary part of the learning process. Ultimately, they are more open to learning because they believe that even their most essential qualities can be developed through training and effort.

On the other hand, the gifts-oriented crowd who believe in the fixed, unchangeable nature of their own traits and qualities are more likely to focus on assignments or projects that they feel comfortable with. They implicitly believe that if you have talent or ability in any area of your life, then everything should come naturally – without effort. When they make mistakes or fail at tasks, they are more likely to feel that it's a sign of lack of ability rather than lack of effort.

Gifts-focused thinkers tend to give up fairly quickly when things go wrong, which is only sensible. After all, if someone really believed that a skill or personal quality was an innate gift and couldn't be upgraded, it would be stupid to keep working at it, right?

As a result, people with more of a growth mind-set have been shown in dozens of studies to perform more strongly than those with a gifts mind-set in all sorts of domains. For example, a survey of business owners found that growth-focused entrepreneurs felt

People with a growth mind-set perform more strongly than those with a gifts mind-set in all sorts of domains.

more resilient and were more confident about taking on challenges than their gifts-focused counterparts.[2] In another study, managers who believed that human attributes could be cultivated and improved were more likely to coach the members of their teams than managers who believed that personal attributes are innate and unalterable.[3]

I can tell you about plenty of studies that have been conducted away from the workplace with similar results too. For instance, adolescent children with a growth mind-set worked harder and had better exam results at school than peers who believed more strongly in their fixed gifts.[4] Women with a growth mind-set about their bodies (i.e. those who believed in the changeability of their bodies) lost weight more successfully than women with a gifts mind-set, who perhaps blamed their circumstances or genes.[5] And students suffering from debilitating levels of shyness tended to become less shy over time if they viewed shyness as something that could be changed as opposed to a fixed trait that they were stuck with.[6]

I'm sure you can see that such results make sense. If any individual truly believed that some aspect of himself or herself could not be changed, then it obviously wouldn't be worth wasting any effort endeavouring to alter it.

Ultimately, the drawback of the gifts mind-set is that it traps people. Those who feel that they are no good at a skill or activity feel it's pointless to try to get better. So they stop trying. They give up, which only guarantees that they can never get better at it.

The gifts mind-set is equally pernicious even for those who've been told that they are a natural at something – that they are better than most people. They may be tempted to believe that they don't need to hunker down and work at it. After all, natural talent doesn't need coaching, training and practice; natural talent doesn't need to identify shortcomings or spot mistakes in order to lift performance even higher.

Those blessed – or should it be cursed? – with true natural talent often coast to early success. But if they get stuck in the rut of the gifts mind-set, they may not learn how to hone their skills further; they don't learn how to cope with setbacks or frustration. They may lose out on the chance to develop their grit and fighting spirit – the ability to dig deep and find the strength to battle on even when things are going wrong.

Reconceptualizing success and failure

Think back to times in your life when others seemed to out-shine you. Perhaps they did better in exams, at sport, in dating and relationships, at work, *anything*. Back then, you may have thought that they were simply more intelligent or had more natural ability.

But now that you understand the gifts versus growth mind-sets, consider the following:

- Did they work harder than you?

- In what ways may they have sought out more (or better) feedback, advice or coaching?

- What kind of different tactics or training strategies may they have used to make more progress?

Your mind-set

So what does all of this mean for you exactly?

Let's head back to those rating scales at the beginning of the chapter. What scores did you give each of those traits and characteristics? Essentially, the higher the scores you gave each attribute, the more you have a growth mind-set about that attribute. And the lower your scores, the more you are currently inclined towards a gifts mind-set.

Your views may have been shaped by the people around you in your upbringing. Perhaps teachers, parents or other adults helpfully encouraged you to work at things (fostering the growth mind-set) or less helpfully told you what you were good at or weren't so good at.

If you're like most people, you probably have a scattering of scores rather than believe that all attributes are either 100 per cent innate or 100 per cent trainable. You doubtless believe that some attributes are more amenable to alteration than others – perhaps you believe that leaders are born rather than made or that public speaking is a skill at which we can all improve (or vice versa).

You can shift your mind-sets and, more importantly, super-charge your motivation and performance.

But it almost doesn't matter which ones you feel you can or can't change – your *current* beliefs are only a starting point. I say current, because the good news is that you can shift your mind-sets and, more importantly, super-charge your motivation and performance. The more you have the growth mentality, the more you will get out of the later chapters of the book when we work through the skills of winning arguments, pitching ideas and so on.

How? What can we do to swing our mind-sets from the gifts end of the spectrum towards the growth end?

For starters, simply reading this chapter will help. Because it turns out that almost nothing about ourselves – at least our psychological characteristics – is immutable. And taking on board this understanding can begin to shift our beliefs.

Experiments have shown that it's possible to alter people's mind-set in mere minutes. In a provocative 2012 study, for example, scientists led by Alexander O'Connor at the University of California, Berkeley, divided a group of university students into two and asked them to read a total of eight quotes on the nature of creativity. Both groups of students read nearly the same list of quotes except for one.

One group was presented with the following as its final quote:

Most artists and supposed creative types just copy someone else. They adjust, tweak a little, but overall it's just the same thing. But some people have some inherent quality that lets them see the bigger picture and do something truly creative.

The second group read this quote instead:

Most artists and supposed creative types just copy someone else. They adjust, tweak a little, but overall, it's just the same thing. But some people work to a point that lets them see the bigger picture and do something truly creative.

When the two groups of students were then asked to complete several tests of creativity, the researchers found that those in the second group were significantly more inventive. In other words, the one sentence had rebooted people's beliefs about the nature of creativity, which subsequently affected their resourcefulness.

The first quote stating that creativity is an "inherent quality" plunged those who read it into the gifts mind-set – it strengthened in them the belief that creativity is simply something you either do or don't have. So, quite unknowingly, they tried less hard on the test of creativity.

Conversely, the second quote stating that "some people work to a point that lets them see the bigger picture and do something truly creative" helped to shift the thinking of the students who read it into the growth mind-set. Consequently, these students actually *became* more sparky and imaginative.[7]

Wow. To me, that's a pretty intoxicating result. It demonstrates that just a single sentence was able to instil in people a superior way of thinking that allowed them to achieve more. So imagine what reading this entire chapter will do for your beliefs and your capacity to achieve.

Experiments have shown that it's possible to alter people's mind-set in mere minutes.

So it's not mere hyperbole to say that our beliefs matter. They *really* matter. Believe that you can change and you will.

Everything changes

Research tells us that change is possible in nearly every area of our lives – even ones that most of society would accept as fairly fixed. For instance, many folks believe that their personalities are fairly established by the time they get into adulthood. However, is that really the case?

Enter Ed Diener, a professor at the University of Illinois at Urbana-Champaign, along with a ground-breaking paper he published in 2006. One of the world's top psychologists, Diener had been measuring the personalities of 1130 adults every two years for an eight-year period. Controversially, he found that people were able to *change* their personalities. By pursuing satisfying work activities and by getting into fulfilling relationships with a significant other, people were able to become more extraverted and less emotionally neurotic.[8]

Early-20th-century academics like Sigmund Freud believed that personality is immutable and doesn't change – or at least without years and years of intensive, expensive therapy. And that widely pervasive view persisted for nearly a century. However, modern 21st-century psychologists such as Diener have demonstrated that self-initiated change is possible.

Now you may expect younger people to change more than older adults. After all, people in their late teens and 20s usually leave home for the first time, find first love, get their first jobs and so on. Everything is shiny and new to younger people – or so you'd think.

But Diener's landmark study showed that this was not the case. He found that people were able to modify their personalities whatever their age. At the start of the eight-year study, his subjects ranged in age from 16 to 70. And those in their 50s or 60s boldly altered their personalities just as much as those in their teens or 20s.

Change isn't something restricted to the young. Old dogs can learn new tricks, it seems.

Shifting mind-set

Simply understanding that the growth mind-set exists (and tends to help people to learn more and ultimately perform better) helps most people to begin thinking about themselves and their skills in a new way. Hopefully you'll begin to see that you can get better at almost anything you want. But if you'd like to take it further and shift your mind-set even more deeply

(*Continued*)

into the growth way of thinking, you might like to work through this exercise.

This is an activity to do over the course of several days. Over the course of five separate days, write at least a couple of paragraphs – or more if you like – answering one of the following questions on each day:

- Can you think of a skill you once weren't very good at but now perform better? This could be a skill you picked up *at any point in your life*. Recalling how you developed your skill, what lessons can you extract about how you learn best?

- Can you think of an instance of someone you know who learnt a new skill? It could be a friend, family member or colleague. Why and how did they change?

- Reflect on a time you overcame a major obstacle or solved a tricky conundrum. How did you manage it? Looking back, what did the experience teach you about how you can help yourself to succeed in future?

- Remind yourself of a different and more recent skill that you've either learnt from scratch or upgraded. What strategies or tactics helped you to improve? And what does it suggest you could do next time you're learning something new?

- Thinking back, can you recall a time you overcame a personal hardship? If you had to tell someone the story of what you did that helped you to succeed, what would you say?

I suggest writing about just the one question per day for a couple of reasons. First, you don't overload yourself with too much. You can focus on quality of thought rather than trying to rush through all five questions at once. In addition, going more slowly allows you to ponder the notion of the growth mind-set longer – and prompt a greater shift in your beliefs – than if you answer all of the questions in a single session.

The potential to grow in whatever we do

How much potential do we have in life? Well, the research on the growth mind-set that we've covered suggests that we may have substantially more room for growth and improvement than we may have been led to believe.

Several years ago, I wrote a book which was initially titled *The Extra One Per Cent*, but it was more recently re-published with the title *E is for Exceptional: The New Science of Success*.[9] I wanted to tell the story of exceptional people and so interviewed dozens of high achievers such as James Averdieck, founder of dessert company Gü Puds, and Josephine Fairley, co-founder of Green & Black's chocolate.

I'm very proud of that book for some of the insights I uncovered. Absurdly, though, I found that many of these thriving entrepreneurs and leaders had been told at school not to strive for their dreams. A few had been told by their teachers that they weren't clever enough. One woman was told that she had no real ability at anything and that her only hope in life would be to land a successful husband! But they all succeeded anyway – with some of them selling their businesses and making millions of pounds in the process.

So don't ever let anyone put you off by telling you that you're not good enough. Just because you may not be very good at something *now* doesn't mean you can't work at it and be good – or even great – at it later.

In my own life, I can think of so many things I've worked at. An example: I've now written more than two dozen books on careers, high achievement and self-improvement – some of which have been translated into dozens of languages and sold to hundreds of thousands of readers worldwide. Sometimes people who don't know me reason that I must be really clever or talented – that writing must be some kind of gift that I possess. But I know the truth.

My first book was less than a third the length of the book you're currently reading but still took me several hundred hours to write. And given that it didn't sell that many copies (mostly because it wasn't terribly good, probably!), it didn't make me very much money. In fact, when I worked out how much I earned from writing it on an hourly basis, I would have earned more if I had washed dishes in a restaurant kitchen or cleaned toilets in a hotel.

But with each book I wrote, I became more methodical in how I researched the topic. I discovered that I write better when I can work from home away from my colleagues and ideally when it's dark outside so the world is quieter and there are fewer distractions. I studied business and self-help books to see how other authors used language and told stories. I scoured magazines ranging from *Wired* to *Men's Health* and *Psychologies* to learn how journalists wrote about research studies. I learnt to pitch my ideas more successfully to bigger publishers and to negotiate better contracts.

And even though I hope that every book I write is a little better, I accept that my writing is a work in progress. The point is: writing books is not a gift that I have always possessed. It's a skill that has grown – that I have honed through lots of hard work. If I had written my first book and believed it was simply a gift that you either had or didn't have, I would have given up.

Learning is possible at any age, whatever a person's upbringing, education or current circumstances.

I believe that most people could write a book if they only put enough work into it. More broadly, I believe that learning is possible at any age, whatever a person's upbringing, education or current circumstances.

My mother – a retired woman in her 60s who looks at least a decade younger – is a wonderful example of this (and my answer to the second question in the "Shifting mind-set" box on page 24). She only got her first computer a couple of years ago and has managed to turn herself into something of a technology guru.

She's an active user of Googlemail, Flickr and Facebook. She takes photos and videos on her digital camera, uploads them to her computer and shares them with friends and family worldwide. She streams music on Spotify and transfers tracks to her Android phone but uses iTunes for managing her iPod Touch. She knows how to navigate her way around her computer and the World Wide Web better than many 20 or 30-somethings!

But there was nothing special about her upbringing that gave her any special advantages: she grew up in a small village in rural China, studied to become a nurse at a hospital in Hong Kong and spent most of her adult years as a full-time, stay-at-home mum. No, the only thing she has is her enquiring mind-set: a willingness to learn, ask questions, try new things and keep growing.

Modifying your mind-set with help from your friends

Research tells us that one major difference that separates those in the growth versus gifts mind-sets is their willingness to ask for help and explore new strategies. So when it comes to be time for you to invest in your self-development, you may want

(Continued)

to interview at least a couple of friends or colleagues who have successfully improved themselves in the same field.

Suppose you're trying to hone your networking skills. Who in your social group are the best networkers? Ask if you can buy them a coffee some time to seek their advice on what they say or do that helps them to be so effective.

If you're aiming to run a marathon next year, sit down with a buddy who has done it to pick up training tips. Or if you yearn to lose weight, quit smoking, write a novel or anything else, again, find your way to a friend – or even a friend of a friend – to ask for practical dos and don'ts. What helped them to achieve the same goal?

Growing your confidence and capabilities

I only came across the growth versus gifts mind-sets a few years ago and it has transformed the way I coach and run leadership training workshops. After all, there's no point training managers in how to become better leaders unless they believe that they *can* change – that they can hone their people management skills, their strategic thinking, their political savvy and so on.

Shifting into a growth mind-set will set you up for the other chapters in this book: to get the most out of putting together winning arguments, constructing clever pitches, getting the job offers you want and ultimately getting ahead. But to finish off, here's a summary of how growth-oriented versus gifts-oriented folks tend to think and behave.[10]

It almost goes without saying: you may want to follow the example of the growth-oriented winners rather than the gifts-minded crowd.

	What do growth-oriented winners do?	What do gifts-oriented people do?
When thinking about themselves	Say: "I am a work in progress."	Say: "I am as good as I'm ever going to get."
When approaching a task	Ask yourself: "How can I get better at this?"	Ask yourself: "Can I do this or not?"
When setting goals	Focus on learning as much about the task or topic as possible because learning is a desirable outcome in its own right.	Focus mainly on outperforming others and/or looking good.
When a task begins to feel tough	Accept that it's only through tackling difficult tasks and projects that we achieve growth.	Give up and focus on easier or entirely different tasks that can be accomplished successfully.
When struggling	Seek advice or help from others; think about further tactics or strategies which may work better.	Feel embarrassed and keep mistakes to themselves; keep working longer rather than trying something different.
When experiencing failure	Accept that glitches and disappointment are necessary on the way to improvement.	Get upset or feel hopeless about the task and want to give up.
When speaking about failure	Say: "I failed at this one task on this occasion but can try again."	Say: "I am a failure and should quit."

(Continued)

	What do growth-oriented winners do?	What do gifts-oriented people do?
When receiving feedback	Actively ask questions to seek out criticism about what could be done better.	Dodge criticism or seek out only positive comments and praise.
When being criticized	Thank the other person for the criticism and try to extract the lessons from the criticism.	Get defensive, make excuses or go on the offensive to criticize the other person.
When praising others	Say: "I notice you did well at that. That tells me you are working hard at it!"	Say: "I notice you did well at that. That tells me you're a natural at it!"

Remember that growth is possible in just about every area of our lives. Pretty much every skill – from public speaking to sporting performance, assertiveness to dealing with numbers – can be improved if you set out to learn. No matter what teachers or other adults may have said in the past; no matter what colleagues, friends or even you yourself may currently say about your weaknesses or limitations, trust the research.

Slipping back into gifts-oriented thinking

Some people don't even realize they're stuck in the rut of the gifts mind-set. A few months ago I was brought into a law firm to coach a world-weary 40-something IT support manager, whom I'll call Keith. He had worked his whole career on computer systems and software, including more than seven years at the law firm, but his performance had deteriorated in the last year or so.

His performance wasn't so terrible that his boss wanted to fire him. But his boss had tried to talk to him and support him, without success.

When I first met Keith, he was only able to muster a wan and fairly unconvincing smile. He revealed that a part of the strain and the trigger for his current work difficulties was an acrimonious divorce. However, when we delved deeper, it transpired that the nature of his work was also changing radically. The firm was outsourcing more work abroad and altering many of its technical requirements. He was struggling to get to grips with the new ways and methods and, as a consequence, he wasn't staying organized and on top of his work.

On being questioned further about his work, Keith talked about how he couldn't cope and how he didn't have the energy to deal with all of his work and the new technical requirements. He admitted that he was avoiding people and spending more time corresponding via email rather than speaking to them face-to-face. Neither was he asking his colleagues in the technology team for help. In other words, he was stuck in the gifts mind-set.

So I encouraged Keith to think back to earlier, less troubled times in his life when he had acquired new skills and learnt about bleeding-edge technologies. We talked about earlier occasions in his 20-year career when he had coped with corporate changes of direction. We also discussed ways for him to prioritize his work so that he could focus on the big, important projects that would make a super-sized difference to his growth and performance.

Over the course of just a few months, Keith's performance lifted, so much so that his boss remarked upon Keith's visible transformation.

But the point is we may not always realize when we may be stuck in the gifts mind-set. Even if we currently have the growth mind-set, it's possible to lose it when things get tough.

> ## Building your growth mind-set momentum
>
> Here's an additional, final exercise to shift your mind-set if you're ever feeling stuck in a gifts frame of mind. Imagine that a close friend is struggling with a quandary or issue – it could be to do with work, family, sports, anything.
>
> Your friend seems to be stuck in the gifts mind-set. He or she feels that there's nothing more to be done. You hear your friend saying things like, "Maybe I'm just no good at this" and "I'm never going to get this – I should give up."
>
> Now type an email or write a letter to your friend explaining the difference between the gifts and growth modes of thinking. And add some advice on how your friend could make progress with the issue.
>
> An alternative would be to bring to mind a particular pal who is actually grappling with something in life. Offer your support and see whether you can coach him or her out of the gifts mind-set and into growth.
>
> The more clearly you can explain it to someone else, the more you will help to cement the notion of the gifts mind-set in your own head.

Keeping up with the world

When I speak at conferences in front of executives and business leaders, I often ask them whether things are changing faster now than they were as little as 10 or even five years ago. Their answer is always an unequivocal "yes".

The Internet is a prime example of how the world is continuing to transform how we do things. Can you believe that it was only in 2007 that MySpace was the world's most popular social networking website? Of course, Facebook is the current king. But who's to say what will be top of the pile in just a few years' time?

Things change daily in the worlds of technology, media, communication and medicine. Scientists are constantly discovering new things about the human mind as well as the far reaches of the universe. Upstart companies spring up while once-great giants disappear. Today's innovations swiftly become yesterday's news. Even the global balances of political power and cultural influence are shifting evermore noticeably. In this age of bewildering, turbo-charged change, it's worth reminding ourselves that every day can be an education, an opportunity to learn and grow.

I shall finish this chapter with a quote from Alfred Binet, the early-20th-century educational psychologist who famously invented the forerunner of the modern IQ test: "With practice, training, and above all, method, we manage to increase our attention, our memory, our judgement and literally to become more intelligent than we were before." Even though IQ tests are often taken as proof that our gifts are fixed, Binet had the opposite view: that with diligence and effort, we could enhance even our very intelligence.

It's worth reminding ourselves that every day can be an education.

So what would you like to upgrade in your life? And, looking at the table above and the column describing what growth-oriented people do, how will you apply it to your own life?

Onwards and upwards

- Throughout this chapter, we've seen that almost no psychological skills, qualities or characteristics are set in stone. Remember that we may be able to modify even our personality and intelligence through effort and discipline. People who feel that they only have certain limited gifts (and therefore certain fixed flaws) curtail their own development; those with the growth mind-set are much more open to learning and ultimately tend to outperform those who believe in their innate gifts.

- Help yourself to shift away from the gifts mind-set and into the growth way of thinking by re-reading this chapter occasionally and bringing to mind occasions when you improved your own skills.

- Continue to foster the growth mind-set by revisiting past difficulties that you overcame in either your professional or personal life. The more you remind yourself how you grew in the past, the more you will bloom in the future.

- Cultivate the growth mind-set by asking for help as well as for constructive criticism from people who are that little bit better than you. Seek out role models who excel at what you want to improve at and ask their advice too.

- Remind yourself of the superior outlook that growth-oriented winners have when it comes to setting goals, dealing with failure and taking on board criticism. The table on page 29 of this chapter has helped many of my coaching clients in the past and may be a useful summary for you too.

2

Winning the Argument

**The only way to get the best of an
argument is to avoid it.**
Dale Carnegie

Some lessons you learn the hard way. And, boy, did I learn the power of an unbeatable argument the hard way.

I was 25 years old and working for my first employer, a large American management consultancy. One day I happened to read an article in the *Financial Times* written by someone I'll call Geoff, the chairman of a small British firm of business psychologists. I thought the article – about the ways in which egotistical leaders could plunge their companies into chaos – was so stunningly insightful that I immediately wanted to work for this smaller firm.

I did what research I could on Geoff and his business and wrote a speculative letter to him. Less than a fortnight later, I was delighted to be offered an interview with one of the directors who reported to him. There were further rounds of interviews as well as a gruelling day-long assessment centre, but, cutting a long story short, I was finally invited to meet Geoff one-on-one.

I realized that he was going to offer me a job. And so on a crisp autumn morning, I walked into that meeting ready to argue my case and negotiate a big salary increase to what I was currently earning.

But Geoff was clever, oh so clever. Wearing an open, sincere expression, he talked about the opportunities at the firm. He pointed his finger at me and told me how he could see me rising up the ranks because he could sense that I was the kind of star that the firm needed. He said that he was so certain I'd do well that it would be inevitable that they'd be raising my salary within six months and then again after a year.

We eventually reached a deal, and it wasn't until after I'd left the meeting that I realized I'd completely failed in my objectives. Even though I had been prepared to argue my case, Geoff somehow flattered and inspired me so much that I agreed to take the job for exactly the same salary as I was already on!

I was later told by a recruitment expert that I could reasonably have expected a 20 to 30 per cent pay rise. But no, I got nothing. Nada. Zip.

Geoff had totally won me over. He had won the argument.

The skill of winning an argument is universally useful. Who doesn't want to be more influential, more persuasive? The skill is as applicable if you're trying to win over a colleague, client or investor as endeavouring to persuade a friend to give up smoking or a loved one to do more housework. So what is it that makes certain hotshots so successful at negotiating deals, changing minds and winning arguments?

> Who doesn't want to be more influential, more persuasive?

Winning arguments without arguing

When it comes to winning arguments, there's both good news and bad.

Let me start with the bad news first: you can't win arguments.

Huh?

Allow me to explain by presenting a dictionary definition of an argument:

Argument (noun).

1. A heated or undignified exchange of conflicting views.
2. A statement, fact, reason or set of reasons given in support of something.

ORIGIN from Latin: *argumentum*, from the verb *arguere* meaning "make clear, prove".

In everyday speech, we customarily use the word "argument" to refer to the first meaning, the heated exchange of conflicting views, when we talk loudly or even shout or scream at each other. And in this situation, we can never truly win.

Think back to the last time you were in such an argument. It may have been over something at work, like how best to tackle a project or where to go for the annual team dinner. Perhaps it was over something at home – whether you're each doing enough of the housework or whose fault it was that the electricity bill didn't get paid. It may have been a quarrel over something either relatively trivial or monumentally important. But how did you feel? And how do you think the other person felt?

Sure, you may have been able to get the other person or persons to do what you wanted (or maybe they were the ones who won by getting you to do what they wanted). But there were probably raised voices. Perhaps you both talked over each other. Maybe one or both of you said something a little hurtful.

All of that can cause bruised feelings. At best, you may have won grudging compliance with what you wanted rather than gaining wholehearted agreement as to the merits of what you were proposing. And that, to me, isn't truly winning an argument. When one party feels resentful or even a little bitter, it damages the relationship.

So we must, wherever possible, avoid those angry clashes – the blurted-out words, the indignant tone of voice and the turmoil of emotions overwhelming our more sensible selves.

Instead, we must focus on the second definition of the word: on presenting facts and reasons to secure agreement.

I said earlier that there's both bad news and good about winning arguments. And it's true that we can't ever genuinely win arguments that are furious clashes – the "heated or undignified exchange of conflicting views", which is the first definition of the word "argument".

But then there's the good news. We *can* win people over by focusing on the second definition of the word, by presenting "a statement, fact, reason or set of reasons" in an altogether quieter and less animated fashion.

> We can't ever genuinely win arguments that are furious clashes.

What's your style of arguing?

Before we move on, can I suggest a little diagnostic test to see how you tend to approach discussions and disagreements, please?

Read the statements below and respond by ticking the box with the number that corresponds to your behaviour. The best way to rate yourself is to go through the statements fairly quickly. This is for your own benefit, so be as honest with yourself as you can.

	1: almost never	2: not often	3: some-times	4: fairly often	5: very often
1. I am able to say "no" to unreasonable requests.					
2. I look for ways to be helpful to the people I work with.					
3. I feel good about my ability to cope with the unexpected.					
4. I respect the rights of others because I expect others to respect my rights.					
5. I have a good (positive) opinion of myself.					
6. I work well with others and get along with others in groups.					
7. I make up my own mind easily without asking others what they think I should do.					

	1: almost never	2: not often	3: some-times	4: fairly often	5: very often
8. Complimenting the people I'm around comes easily and naturally to me.					
9. I can be very focused or very relaxed whenever I want to be.					
10. I make plans, set goals and try to prepare myself for the future.					
11. I am aware of my feelings and express them in constructive ways.					
12. When someone is explaining something, I try to pay close attention.					
13. I expect to get what I pay for in the marketplace, and I am not easily taken advantage of.					

(Continued)

	1: almost never	2: not often	3: some- times	4: fairly often	5: very often
14. I get started on my regular job or work assignment without needing to be told or reminded.					
15. I feel relaxed and comfortable in social situations.					
16. During meetings or group discussions, I speak up and add my feelings and thoughts on the subject.					
17. I take reasonable risks to achieve my goals.					
18. I say what I think and feel about things. I express my opinion freely.					
19. I am direct and get right to the point.					
20. I feel comfortable with people who are quite different from me in race, background or lifestyle.					

The questionnaire gives us two distinct measures of how we may deal with different interpersonal situations.

To calculate your overall *Respect For Others* score, add up the individual scores you gave to yourself on the even numbered statements 2 through 14 (i.e. 2, 4, 6, 8, 10, 12 and 14). This should give you a total Respect For Others score of between 7 and 35.

To calculate your total *Assertion* score, add up the scores you gave yourself to all of the odd numbered statements 1 through 15 (i.e. 1, 3, 5, 7, 9, 11, 13 and 15). And add to that the scores you gave yourself to questions 16 through to 20 as well. This should give you a total Assertion score of between 14 and 70.

If you like, you can write your scores in here:

Respect For Others =
Assertion =

The questionnaire was developed by University of Arkansas scholars Ed Williams and Robert Akridge. The fact that it was developed by academics means that the test is rigorous and robust (i.e. it provides us with quite a lot of insight into how adults tend to behave in vexing interpersonal situations).[1]

Once we know how you currently tend to go about influencing people, we can look at the right strategies to help you to get better at it.

Of course, once we know how you currently tend to go about influencing people, we can look at the right strategies to help you to get better at it. To gauge how you stack up against other folks, take a look at the tables below.

Your Respect For Others score	Implication
35	When dealing with others, you show a great deal of respect for others – more so than 95 per cent of people
33	You show a good deal of respect – more than 75 per cent of people
31	You show average levels of consideration for others – 50 per cent of people are more respectful than you but 50 per cent are less respectful
29	You could show more levels of consideration for others – 75 per cent of people show *more* respect for others than you do
27	You could show considerably more respect for others – 85 per cent of people tend to show *more* respect for others than you do

Your Assertion score	Implication
62	When dealing with others, you assert yourself exceedingly strongly – more so than 95 per cent of people
57	You assert yourself quite strongly – more than 75 per cent of people
52	You show average levels of assertion – 50 per cent of people are more assertive than you but 50 per cent are less assertive
48	You could be more assertive – 75 per cent of people are *more* assertive than you
44	You could be quite a lot more assertive – 85 per cent of people are *more* assertive than you

Once you have both of your scores, you can plot your influencing style using the grid below. If you scored 33 or above on Respect For Others, that's a high score. A score of around 31 is average. A score of 29 or lower would be considered low.

In terms of Assertion, a score of 57 or above is high. Around 52 is average. And 48 or lower would be considered low.

For instance, an individual scoring 28 on Respect For Others and 63 on Assertion would be classified as demonstrating mainly Forceful Persuasion. Someone else scoring 31 on Respect For Others and 47 on Assertion would be somewhere between Passivity and Helpfulness.

So what's your current style for convincing and cajoling people?

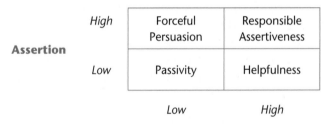

		Low	High
Assertion	*High*	Forceful Persuasion	Responsible Assertiveness
	Low	Passivity	Helpfulness

Respect For Others

Understanding what your interpersonal style says about you

I like to think of effective influencing as about both give and take in equal measure. Respect For Others is about giving – giving other people the chance to express their views, for example. On the other hand, Assertion is about taking – swooping in on opportunities in situations and asserting our rights to take from those situations what we desire.

Ideally, we want to score highly on both Respect For Others and Assertion. But as you can see from the grid above, it's possible to be high on Respect For Others but low on Assertion (which results in the Helpfulness style of influencing) or high on Assertion but low on Respect For Others (which results in the Forceful Persuasion style). The fourth combination is to be low on both Respect and Assertion, which results in Passivity.

Here's a brief guide to how people who display each of the four influencing styles tend to behave and be perceived by others.

Helpfulness

Helpfulness is the trademark of people who are high on Respect For Others but low on Assertion. As you can no doubt guess, individuals who have the Helpfulness style are great team players. They are often courteous, likeable and friendly. They tend to be good listeners and have wonderful empathy for the problems and issues facing others.

The fact that individuals with this style have a high level of Respect For Others is a fantastic strength, but the fact that it's coupled with low Assertion can mean that others may take advantage of them. Researchers at Columbia University have coined a phrase to describe such individuals: they could be perceived as "instrumentally impotent" (i.e. less able to achieve their own goals).[2]

A buddy of mine, I'll call Arun, definitely tends towards Helpfulness. A slim Indian guy with a tendency to drop eye contact when he speaks, he's a software engineer who is always busy because his colleagues are constantly asking him for help with their projects.

He has been told repeatedly that he knows more about his field of expertise than most of his colleagues and even many of the managers in his department. But he has seen others being promoted above him because he doesn't put himself forward. He believes in talking only when he has something to say and his voice is repeatedly drowned out by some of his louder, more aggressive colleagues.

Arun comes across as agreeable and friendly, which are of course good traits. At the same time, though, he is perhaps too deferential. The fact that he rarely speaks up is sadly interpreted as meaning that he doesn't have anything to contribute.

He would like to advance in his career but he doesn't do a very good job of telling his bosses what he wants and why he should get it. Arguably, his biggest problem is that he doesn't say "no" frequently enough to the more trivial requests that are made of him, which means that he doesn't have the time to pursue the greater opportunities that could help him to vault up the career ladder.

Is your main influencing style Helpfulness?

Forceful Persuasion

People who are high on Assertion but lower on Respect For Others can be said to utilize the Forceful Persuasion interpersonal style. These individuals tend to be good at speaking their minds, stating their case and telling others what they want. They often get it too – at least in the short term.

They tend to see themselves as being direct and uncompromis-ing – they don't pull punches. However, others may find them a little too pushy, sometimes abrasive or even aggressive, which may damage longer-term relationships. The same crew at Columbia University describe such individuals as "socially insufferable".

A client of mine, let's call her Tatiana, used to be known for her Forceful Persuasion style. The managing partner of a tax advisory firm, with blue-grey eyes and long, straight blonde hair falling down her back, she had been encouraged by her colleagues to seek coaching on her leadership style. When she got in touch with me, I began by interviewing some of her team to find out what they thought her strengths and weaknesses were. They described her as someone who was fiercely determined. Once she set her mind on something, she rarely gave in until she got her way. Her colleagues always knew where they stood with her too: she never shied away from condemning the faults with a project or a colleague's work.

While they admired Tatiana's strengths, they also pointed out that she could at times be quite inflexible or even intimidating. They felt that she didn't seem to listen to or value others' opinions, for instance on a couple of occasions she seemed to listen only to disregard totally what she heard. They also said that, while she was quick to point out faults, flaws and mistakes, she rarely praised good work or thanked people for their efforts.

Thankfully, Tatiana was willing to work on her interpersonal style in order to lift her effectiveness as a leader. Over the course of less than a year, she made considerable strides in improving her empathy and listening skills. She got much better at complimenting and acknowledging people's efforts and finding more sensitive ways to phrase her criticisms.

Passivity

People who are low on both Assertion and Respect For Others may end up with the Passivity interpersonal style. Their lower Assertion means that they feel less comfortable speaking up and asking for what they want – even if their goals are perfectly reasonable. But at the same time, their inability to show greater Respect means that they can be ignored by those around them. Individuals who have the Passivity style often feel a little isolated or frustrated that they aren't taken more seriously by others.

I was once recruited to coach a lawyer who exhibited the Passivity style. With the constantly furrowed brow of a deep thinker, Jarrod was a highly competent technical specialist: he had a magnificent amount of knowledge about the specifics of real-estate law. However, his colleagues complained that he seemed to be in his own private world. They said that he didn't really tell them what he was working on – it often seemed as if he was working on projects that interested him rather than assignments that would be of the most use to the wider firm. Neither did he respond promptly enough to his colleagues' requests for assistance. In other words, people felt that he wasn't enough of a team player.

When I first met Jarrod, he explained that he frequently felt thwarted by his own inability to speak up. Even when he did speak up, he tended to do so indirectly by hinting and alluding to issues rather than broaching them unambiguously. As a result, his ideas and suggestions rarely got taken on board by his colleagues.

He knew *what* he wanted to achieve in terms of being taken more seriously. He longed to develop his gravitas and personal impact so that he could have a greater say in how the team operated. However, he couldn't initially see *how* he could achieve it.

Responsible Assertiveness

People who influence using the Responsible Assertiveness style both demonstrate respect for others and manage to assert their own rights. It's worth aspiring to develop the Responsible Assertiveness style, as researchers have found that this influencing style helps people to deal most successfully with stressful events.[3]

Being responsibly assertive means being able to give and take in a balanced fashion. Individuals who are respectful but unassertive tend to give too much of their time and risk having their own goals and desires unfulfilled. People who are assertive without showcasing sufficient respect tend to take too frequently and may be perceived as pushy or abrasive.

I came across a chief executive by the name of Angela who was a shining example of Responsible Assertiveness. One of only a few women in a bullish, male-dominated engineering business, she wasn't afraid of speaking her mind and making tough decisions. When the company was hit by a prolonged sales slump, she realized that she needed to make some of her workforce redundant. The workers were heavily unionized, so she faced stiff resistance, but she was mentally strong enough to press forward with her plans.

At the same time, though, she displayed great empathy for the employees who were to lose their jobs without ever being patronizing. She took a lot of time to talk to them individually, listening to their worries and fears, and discussing other career options and dispensing job-hunting advice. By being so supportive, she was able to make a brutal situation as tolerable as possible.

Angela was both able to do what she needed to do for the business but at the same time demonstrate that she cared about people and empathized with their plights. She managed those around her with a vigorous combination of both heart and head. Or, putting it another way, she displayed high levels of both Respect For Others and Assertion.

Developing your influencing style

Remember from our discussion of the growth mind-set in Chapter 1 that our skills are not fixed forever. None of our talents is set in stone. The questionnaire diagnoses your *current* style of arguing to give you an inkling of how you may need to develop.

All of us could be better, though. Even if you already tend to use the Responsible Assertiveness style, bear in mind that even experts can learn, grow and improve.

The questionnaire diagnoses your *current* style of arguing to give you an inkling of how you may need to develop.

Learning from others

One of the best ways to develop your influencing style is to observe others who are currently better at it than you. So who in either your work environment or social circle has the flair you desire?

For example, if you have a high Respect For Others score but a low Assertion score, look around you for people who are good at taking what they want. You might feel that some of their tactics wouldn't suit you, but are there any that would?

Or if you currently have a lower Respect For Others score, cast around for role models who seem to have good listening skills, who demonstrate empathy and care for others. If you see them using particular phrases or see them behaving in certain ways – maybe it's their tone of voice or body language – then see if you can adapt it and adopt it into your repertoire.

In the remainder of this chapter, I'll outline specific techniques that may help you to work on becoming more effective at negotiating and influencing others. Some of the tips are more useful to those who are low on Assertion. Other pointers are more aimed at those who are lower on Respect For Others. But if you find yourself being low on both Assertion and Respect For Others, you may find all of the advice useful.

Improving your influence: Understanding what it means to be assertive

People who score lower on the questionnaire measure of Assertion (regardless of whether they're high or low on Respect For Others) can sometimes find it difficult to communicate what they want because they aren't sure that they have the right to speak up. So an inaugural step to becoming more effective at winning arguments is to take on board what it means to be more assertive.[4]

There's no single definition of what makes up assertive behaviour, but many therapists and researchers have included the following as some of its components:

- Being able to say "no" when you want to (rather than saying "yes" to please others).

- Being able to say "yes" when you want to (rather than feeling obliged to say "no", again perhaps to please others).

- Being able to tell others how you feel – to express your feelings in a confident (but not aggressive) manner.

- Being able to make reasonable requests and set clear boundaries on important issues – and defend them – even though it may cause conflict.

If you're lower on Assertion, can you think of situations in which you could have displayed one of the four assertive behaviours from the bullet list above?

Improving your influence: Taking the time to prepare

Some people who score lower on the measure of Assertion (again, regardless of whether they're high or low on Respect For Others) don't grasp what it means to be assertive. However, research tells us that the majority of people who are lower on Assertion *understand* the correct hypothetical response but find it hard to deliver it – they find it difficult to communicate their desires as opposed to misunderstanding that they have the right to speak up.[5]

If that's the case: enough! It's time to take control.

One helpful tip if you're lower on Assertion is simply to prepare what you'd like to say. Clearly, if you want to ask a colleague or your boss for something, you can prepare ahead of time to assemble a well-crafted argument, choose the right words and even rehearse what you wish to say. But what if someone should pounce on you, asking for something that you don't know how to say "no" to?

> One helpful tip if you're lower on Assertion is simply to prepare what you'd like to say.

Years ago, a friend of mine remarked on several occasions that she always only came up with clever ripostes to other people's arguments after the fact. So I suggested that, rather than trying to argue her case there and then each time, she should ask for a "time out" to allow her to muster her thoughts.

Many people who don't necessarily think quickly on their feet could do with asking for a "time out". When someone asks you for help or a favour, reply straightaway by saying that you would like a little time – it could be a few minutes or a day or more – to get back to them. Just because people ask you to do things that *they* feel are important doesn't mean that you don't have things to do that are *more* worthy of your time.

If a colleague asks you whether you'd mind staying late to help with her project, you might say something like: "Let me finish what I'm doing and I'll come back to you in five minutes." That gives you the time to consider your priorities. Is her project something you really want to be doing? What other things might you feel were more critical?

To help you to construct your own ways of deflecting people's questions and asking for a time out, consider some further examples:

- "I don't know if I'll be free later yet. Let me see how I get on with my own work and I'll let you know my thoughts this afternoon."

- "I'm quite surprised by that and I don't know what to say about it yet. Let me go away and I promise I'll come back before lunchtime with a more considered response."

- "That's a big question and I'm not sure how I feel at the moment. I'd like to mull it over and get back to you about it at the end of the week. What time on Friday would be the best time to speak again?"

Hitting the pause button

Your turn. You will feel most comfortable asking for a time out if you have a phrase that you feel 100 per cent comfortable using. So look at the examples and come up with your own now:

-

It may feel difficult at first to ask for thinking time, but it gets easier with practice. Try it.

Improving your influence: Applying the DEAR formula

People who score lower on Assertion may struggle to find the right words to communicate what they're thinking. They may worry that the wrong words could lead to a quarrel. But the DEAR acronym sets out a simple method for choosing the right words to say.

The four steps are as follows:

- **Describe** the facts of the situation objectively – start with facts and figures or impartial observations if possible.

- **Express** your opinions, rights or feelings – talk about what you're thinking or how a situation is making you feel.

- **Acknowledge** the other person's perspective: empathize with how the other person may be feeling. What might their concerns be?

- **Recommend** a solution (or recommend joint problem-solving): finally, talk about what you want. Or, perhaps because you're not sure what the resolution to a problem may be, suggest that you work together to discuss options and choose a solution together.

For example, suppose that you have performed well on all of your assignments at work and are now hankering for your boss to give you more responsibility. Your DEAR case may go along the following lines:

- Describe the facts of the situation objectively: "I'm sure you can see that I've exceeded all of my targets and objectives over the course of the last year."

- Express your opinions, rights or feelings: "I feel I'm now ready to take on a larger project with more responsibility and a larger budget too."

- Acknowledge the other person's perspective: "I appreciate that you may feel nervous about giving me more responsibility."

- Recommend a solution (or recommend that you both work on a solution together): "But I'm not suggesting that you give me a bigger project and leave me entirely alone. Perhaps it would make sense for us to have weekly check-up meetings about the project to begin with."

Or suppose that you have a long-standing commitment to go out one evening to celebrate a loved one's birthday. A colleague asks you at short notice to stay late to help with a project that you think isn't remarkably urgent. Your DEAR response could go something like:

- Describe the facts of the situation objectively: "On this particular evening, I've already got plans."

- Express your opinions, rights or feelings: "I've already committed to going out to celebrate someone's birthday."

- Acknowledge the other person's perspective: "I appreciate that you feel overloaded."

- Recommend a solution (or recommend that you both try to think of a solution together): "But perhaps there are other people who could help you with it – or I could help you with it tomorrow morning if that's any use."

No one claims that the DEAR approach will allow you to present your case elegantly and eloquently. But if you struggle with getting your point across, it can be a handy starting point. You may feel a little awkward the first handful of times you apply it, but most people who deploy it find that they get better quite rapidly with practice.

Articulating your arguments

Role playing is a powerful method for learning or honing skills. Pretend that you have been confronted with each of the situations below. Using the DEAR acronym, how would you deal with each? If you like, you could write down your responses. But if you wanted to get the biggest boost to your assertiveness skills, ask friends if they would mind letting you practise speaking your requests out loud to them.

Try working through each of the following:

- Your boss seems to be giving all of the menial and boring tasks to you rather than sharing them around the team more equally.

- You're in a restaurant having dinner. Unfortunately, the waiter brings over a plate of food that has gone cold.

- You're struggling to complete an assignment. One of your colleagues doesn't seem overly busy and you suspect that she could help.

- You feel that the person you live with is not contributing enough to the household chores.

So how about putting DEAR into practice? Think about a specific situation in which the DEAR technique could help you to assert yourself. Have a go at writing out your responses under each of the four headings. Then practise saying them out loud a couple of times until you feel comfortable enough to have a go for real.

Improving your influence: Engaging in counterfactual thinking

Here's a final proven technique for you if you happen to score lower on Assertion (irrespective of whether you're high or low on Respect For Others). University of California business school researcher Laura Kray and her colleagues conducted several experiments looking at how different types of preparation could help people who were about to engage in a business negotiation.

Learning from experience often involves thinking about previous situations and reflecting on how we could have done things otherwise. Kray and her colleagues asked groups of business negotiators to engage in one of two discrete types of reasoning about the past:

- Additive counterfactual thinking: deliberating about things that they wished they *had* done, for example, "If only I had made my request earlier" or "If only I had listened more instead of talking so much." It's called additive counterfactual thinking because effectively it's thinking about actions they wish they had added into a previous agreement.

- Subtractive counterfactual thinking: mulling over things that they wished they had *not* done (i.e. activities they wished they could have subtracted or removed from a previous deal). Examples could include, "If only I had not talked so quickly" or "If only I had not lost my temper."

In two separate experiments, Kray and her team found that one of these two forms of counterfactual thinking resulted in significantly improved negotiation performance.[6] One involved thinking about actions that negotiators wished they *had* taken; the other involved actions they wished they had *not* taken. Care to guess which one was the more beneficial?

The answer: the researchers found that additive counterfactual thinking gave negotiators a measurable advantage. In other words, it pays to spend some time before a discussion reminding yourself about a previous transaction and what you wished you had done, what you could have added to the conversation.

It almost goes without saying – it sounds like common sense – that preparation and planning would help us to assert ourselves and bargain more effectively. But I like the finding by Kray and her team because it tells us an unreservedly specific way in which we can be using our preparation time.

> It pays to spend some time before a discussion reminding yourself about a previous transaction and what you wished you had done.

Identifying past flaws and foibles

The next time you want to have an effective, assertive discussion, take a few minutes to engage in some counterfactual thinking. This exercise is adapted from the paper published by Kray and colleagues.

At the end of a discussion or negotiation, people often have thoughts like "if only", in that they can see how things might have turned out better. For instance, if you're having a discussion with a colleague, you may think, "If only I had stated my request a bit more loudly" or "If only I had brought my notes with me to prompt me through the discussion." Often, we wish we had done something extra to achieve a better outcome.

Spend a few minutes now listing *three* specific actions that in retrospect you could have taken to improve your performance in a specific discussion. Each thought you list must start with the phrase "If only I had . . ."

(Continued)

So write out three sentences beginning with the phrase:

- If only I had . . .
- If only I had . . .
- If only I had . . .

Once you've done that, you'll give yourself the best chance of having a firm but positive discussion.

Finally, remember that this technique has been verified by science. When can you give it a go?

Improving your influence: Understanding the need for understanding

We will come shortly to the first tactic specifically geared towards those individuals who may score lower on the questionnaire measure of Respect For Others – and especially for those who are also currently higher on Assertion. Being more respectful is of particular importance when we need to deal with the same individuals over and over again. If we only need to interact with someone – possibly a colleague from an overseas department or a supplier – on a one-off basis, we can probably get away with coming across as quite pushy in order to get what we want. Why should we care if they feel a bit bruised and battered by an exchange?

But if we need to deal with colleagues in our own team, regular clients or even friends and family, then being forceful could cost us in the long-term. Sure, they may do as we want a couple of times, but ultimately they may come to resent us, perhaps looking for ways to undermine us or warn others not to deal with us.

I once coached a newly promoted 35-year-old marketing manager I'll call Neil who was fantastic at designing campaigns and negotiating with advertising agencies. He had a reputation for wearing beautifully tailored suits that showed off his trim physique, but was regrettably better known as a boss who was stubborn and overbearing with his team. But with a concerted effort on his part over the course of six months, his team reported noticeable adjustments in his willingness to compromise.

The secret to his transformation? He altered how he ran one-to-one meetings with the members of his team: he began by asking more questions and taking notes. Only after paraphrasing what he thought he'd heard did Neil then start to talk about what he wanted his team to do. It wasn't that he hadn't been willing to be less stubborn and domineering; like many people who are lower on Respect For Others, he'd never truly realized how much of an issue it had been or what to do about it.

Now I'm sure you've heard how important it is to listen to other people. It's a message we've heard time and again. But when we're trying to get our own points across, how often do we *really* listen and take on board what others are saying? The truth is that we frequently don't do it to the extent that we could.

Think about it another way: simply telling others to do what we want rarely works. Telling them what we want from them or how they need to change doesn't tend to get results. It's only when people first feel that they have been understood – that they have shared their opinions, grievances and feelings *and* had them taken on board – that they can be receptive to what we may have to say.

> How often do we *really* listen and take on board what others are saying?

61

Improving your influence: Helping others to *feel* understood

This particular technique for bolstering our Respect For Others involves both what psychologists call perspective-giving and perspective-taking. But in plain English, that simply means giving others the opportunity to talk (letting them engage in perspective-giving) and then summarizing to *demonstrate* that we understand what they said (engaging in explicit perspective-taking).

Cognitive scientists Emile Bruneau and Rebecca Saxe at the famed Massachusetts Institute of Technology have tested the effects of perspective-giving and perspective-taking amongst groups that have traditionally had fiendishly adversarial relationships, such as Israelis and Palestinians in the Middle East. In one study, for example, they video-recorded discussions between white Americans (who were opposed to immigration) and Mexican immigrants.

The scientists first invited the Mexican immigrants to describe the difficulties that they faced in their societies. The Americans then had to summarize as accurately as possible what they had been told by the Mexicans.

When the researchers then asked each of the two groups to rate their attitudes towards the other group, they found that the intervention improved both groups' attitudes to each other. Feeling heard made the Mexicans rate the Americans as less ignorant and selfish. And listening made the Americans rate the Mexicans as more thoughtful and honest.[7]

A critic could argue that the study only confirms what we knew all along. That it's common sense that listening matters.

But my observation is that so-called common sense is often uncommonly put into action. The lesson is clear: when we yearn to change other people's minds, we must not only listen but also *demonstrate* that we have listened. When we help others to *feel* heard, we help to restore their dignity with the result that they warm to us and may be more amenable to our requests too. Or, as American journalist Abigail van Buren once said: "The less you talk, the more you're listened to."

> **When we yearn to change other people's minds, we must not only listen but also *demonstrate* that we have listened.**

Applying a framework for listening

As I mentioned, I'm sure you've probably heard on more than one occasion the importance of listening to what others have to say. But why don't we do it?

The simple truth is that we get caught up in our own objectives – what we want from a discussion – rather than thinking about the other party being a person (or persons) with wants and needs too. When I'm training clients in better listening and negotiation skills, the key to success seems to centre on taking notes. The next time you're having a slightly contentious discussion or negotiation with someone, try following these steps:

- Begin by sharing your point of view briefly. For instance, if you requested the meeting, you may wish to state your case for a promotion, more responsibility or whatever else you want.

- Next, **ask questions** to find out the other person's perspective, for example, "How do you feel about this?", "What's your take on the situation?" and "I'm not saying that I can give you everything you want, but what would you ideally want from this discussion?"

(Continued)

- Then listen to the responses and **take comprehensive notes**. If you can't get everything down, ask the other person to slow down: "I don't want to miss anything, so could you repeat that for me again please?"

- Keep taking notes until the other person has run out of things to say. Steer clear of the temptation to jump in to refute any of the other person's claims yet.

- Next, read your notes and **summarize out loud what you think the other person said**. Check that you've understood correctly by using phrases like "If I've understood correctly, you said that . . ."

The really key steps (in bold) are asking questions, taking notes and then repeating back what's been said. A lot of people ask questions but only the exceptional few make the concerted effort to write the answers down and then summarize them.

Only when you have paraphrased everything that you think you heard should you proceed with the rest of the discussion. Then you could build your case by using the DEAR method (see Improving your influence: Applying the DEAR formula, on page 55).

Asking questions and taking notes doesn't sound particularly difficult, right? And you're right that it's not *intellectually* difficult. We can all grasp the need. It's *putting it into practice* – going against years of habit – that requires diligence and effort.

Researchers such as Deborah Ancona at MIT's Sloan School of Management distinguish between listening (which she calls "inquiring": actively asking questions to comprehend the thoughts and feelings of others) versus telling (which she calls "advocating": talking about your opinions).[8] If there's a common fault, it's that people who are lower on Respect tend to do more telling/advocating than listening/inquiring.

You *can* change your style. The only question is: will you?

Improving your influence: Adopting both/and thinking

In life we often categorize the people and situations we encounter. It makes life easier to be able to say that someone is either one thing or another. John is creative while Lucy is not. Patrick is shy while Rosanna talks too much. Neela is careful while Alicia cuts corners. I am right and you are wrong.

It's a trap that many of us fall into – and not just those who tend to be lower on the questionnaire measure of Respect For Others. But to describe people in such sweeping terms is more often than not an oversimplification. People are rarely either entirely one thing or wholly something else. In reality, most of humanity – and that includes ourselves – can be *both* one thing *and* another.

> People are rarely either entirely one thing or wholly something else.

It may be that John has *both* some exquisite ideas *and* more than a few stupid ones; Lucy may be *both* not very creative at work *and* creative in her home life; Patrick may be *both* shy around strangers *and* a chatterbox with close confidantes; Rosanna may *both* talk too much *and* yet be insecure deep-down at the same time.

Almost all of us are driven by a mix of different motives. At times we may behave in one way, but occasionally we may lapse and do the precise opposite. For example, while most people would never steal from a friend, surveys show that many cheat on their taxes and effectively steal from the government.[9] Most people try to act calmly and to treat others fairly but can find themselves occasionally losing their temper, sulking or behaving a bit selfishly.

People are complex creatures, and it's a good idea to remember that we can be *both* one thing *and* another. People can both be organized at work and yet disorganized at home. They may be both unassuming with some colleagues and yet forthcoming with other colleagues or clients. They may even behave mostly one way in meetings but then surprise people by doing the precise opposite on another day.

Challenging your own thinking

What either/or distinctions have you made about the people in your life? Perhaps you think of some individuals as helpful and other people as not. Or some people as friends and others as enemies.

Can you think of ways in which you can de-categorize such distinctions using the idea of both/and? For instance, suppose that you have a colleague called Owen who seems to be rather uncooperative. Try reconceptualizing him as someone who is *both* unhelpful to you *and* helpful to at least certain others. Once you can hold those seemingly contradictory concepts in your mind, you can start to think about how Owen's relationships with those other people differ.

What is it that those other colleagues do that makes Owen so much more amenable and helpful? Once you have the answer to that question, you may be able to act on getting Owen to help you out more too.

Have a think now about some of the key people in your life. What boxes have you put them in? What either/or labels have you applied to their behaviour or personalities?

Thinking in terms of either/or limits our ability to deal with people and new situations. Either/or tries to simplify a messy, jagged world that in actuality isn't easily categorized. In order to deal with people and uncharted situations successfully, we must not only tolerate complexity but also actively revel in both/and.

All of this is of particular importance when we're not getting on well with others or trying to argue a case. If we're in a dispute with others, it's rarely the case that we are entirely right and the other party completely wrong.

In order to deal with people and uncharted situations successfully, we must not only tolerate complexity but also actively revel in both/and.

Consider a case of a manager, Gwen, who is disciplining her employee Kieran for repeatedly turning up to work late. Gwen may feel that she is right because Kieran has failed to perform his duties satisfactorily.

But Kieran may feel that he is doing the right thing in being late to work because it's more important for him to get his son to school safely every day. Perhaps he feels morally justified in turning up to work late because he hates Gwen's bullying style of management and is trying to preserve his own sanity. Or he feels that he is in the right to turn up late because he stays late most evenings.

Either/or thinking promotes a black-and-white, overly simplistic way of looking at situations: if I'm right, then you *must* be wrong. But in many situations, it turns out that both parties can be both somewhat right and somewhat wrong.

Even if I am technically in the right because of certain laws, regulations or rules, it's possible that you may still feel morally right or emotionally vindicated to behave the way you do. The most effective negotiators accept that both/and is invariably the more realistic way of looking at situations in our sometimes mind-bogglingly complex world.

Accepting that *both* you *and* others can be right at the same time

If you're stuck in a squabble with someone, remember that *both* of you can be right *and* the other person can feel right or at least justified in his or her behaviour too. Even if you are totally certain that the other person is mainly to blame for a situation, consider that you may *also* have contributed to it – either by your action or inaction.

Before you decide to discuss a sensitive or difficult matter, ask yourself: "Either by my action *or* inaction, how may *I* have inadvertently contributed to this situation?"

I'm sure you can see how keeping the notion of both/and in mind is a vital component of winning people over. But it's likewise an important way of thinking when it comes to our careers too. For example, we'll see that office politics is not entirely bad or good. You can both play politics and have good motives. More on that in Chapter 5: Winning the Race.

Improving your influence: Changing the name of the game

What kind of game do you think you are playing when you're having a discussion or negotiation? People who are high on Assertion but lower on Respect For Others often think of negotiations as what's known as a "fixed-pie game".

Allow me to explain. A fixed-pie game is one in which the benefits are like a freshly baked pie of a certain size. If one person called John takes three-quarters of the pie, then obviously Jane can only take a maximum of one-quarter of the pie. If John were to grab more of the pie – say he gets 85 per cent of the pie, then it must mean taking more from Jane. She can only end up with a maximum of 15 per cent of the pie.

However, many negotiations are not fixed-pie games. For instance, say two people are haggling over the terms of a promotion. Paul is asking for £90,000 a year as his basic salary but his would-be boss, Theresa, is only able to offer a maximum of £85,000. So in terms of money, it may indeed be the case that there is a limited amount of metaphorical pie. For Paul to win, Theresa has to lose by taking money out of some other budget. Or for Theresa to win, Paul has to lose by agreeing to take less.

But there may be other concessions, allowances or deals that either person could make. Theresa could ask Paul to accept a lower salary but offer him every Friday afternoon off from work. She could perhaps encourage him to accept the lower salary in return for being able to hire and fire and put together the perfect team without interference from her.

Paul could ask for the higher salary but agree to take on an additional task or responsibility which would really help Theresa out. Or he could ask for the higher salary but agree to save Theresa money by putting it in writing that he would only ever travel by economy class rather than business class.

Going back to our pie analogy, thinking about those broader concessions and proposals is like thinking first about a way to bake a bigger pie before deciding how to share it out.

Why does this matter?

Research, of course. Nir Halevy, a rising star of a professor at Stanford University, has found that people's perceptions about the games that they think they are playing change their behaviour. If we believe that we are fighting over who can take away the biggest slice of a fixed-pie, then of course we may come across as more combative. In order for me to win more, you have to lose.

But if we can alter our thinking and conceive of discussions as opportunities to work together to first bake a larger pie before divvying it up, we may be able to broker terms that end up being better for both parties. The additional benefit from Halevy's research is that people who think of the game as bake-a-bigger-pie-*then*-share-it-out also tend to come across as more helpful, friendly, kind and trustworthy.[10]

People's perceptions about the games that they think they are playing change their behaviour.

Thinking in terms of collaboration and compromise

Simply understanding the difference between a fixed-pie game and a bake-a-bigger-pie-then-share-it-out game may already help us to behave more cooperatively and less aggressively. To further encourage this shift in your thinking, chew over the following questions before going into any discussion or negotiation:

- What steps can I take in order to make this more of a cooperative rather than combative discussion?

- What steps could I suggest that we take *together* to reach the best, mutually beneficial agreement possible?

- What concessions, allowances or compromises would I be willing to trade off?

- What additional concessions, allowances or compromises could I ask for?

Improving your influence: Keeping our emotions in check

Here's a final tip for all of us.

But first, a question: how would you describe your voice? Calm and unruffled? Enthusiastic and energetic? Anxious and apprehensive? There are lots of ways in plain English of describing how we speak. But scientists use the term "prosody" to refer to speech features such as stress, intonation and rhythm. For example, if you have a voice that has a large dynamic range – which varies, say, from a whisper to a shout on a regular basis – your voice would be said to have a high degree of prosodic emphasis.

Parents often speak to their babies with exaggerated prosodic emphasis. They speak quietly and then more loudly; they allow their voice to range from rumbling bass notes to soaring squeaks. And they do all of this possibly because it may help infants to understand speech.[11] But what's good for talking to babies may not be so good when we're trying to influence others or argue our case.

In a study written up in the prestigious *Journal of Applied Psychology*, researchers Jared Curhan and Alex Pentland at the Massachusetts Institute of Technology asked experimental participants to assume the roles of either an employer or a candidate in a recruitment scenario. The employer's role was to hire the candidate for as little cost as possible. Clearly, the candidate's aim was to get the best compensation package possible.

Observing many dozens of negotiations, the researchers found that people who demonstrated *more* emphasis in their voices tended to perform *less* well. Being emphatic was a liability in the discussions, irrespective of whether the participant was the employer or the candidate. Even more startlingly, the investigators only measured prosodic emphasis during the first five minutes of the transaction.[12]

Why? Why should initial emphasis – a more dynamic voice – lead to worse negotiation outcomes?

We typically use emphasis – sometimes deliberately but more often inadvertently – to convey emotion. We speak more loudly or shout when we're angry. Our voices may become more high-pitched when we're excited or waver when we're unnerved. Therefore, the use of emotion may betray the importance we attach to the issues we're discussing – especially during those early minutes of the conversation when we're sizing each other up.

The use of emotion may betray the importance we attach to the issues we're discussing.

So. The moral: stay calm. Don't enter into a discussion over an issue when you're feeling excited, unhappy or outraged about it. Wait until you can view the situation from a cooler, more detached perspective; otherwise, your voice may inadvertently give you – and the game – away.

Putting it all together

Winning arguments isn't a skill that comes overnight. But it is a skill. And it can be honed, developed and cultivated over time.

Winning arguments isn't a skill that comes overnight. But it is a skill. And it can be honed, developed and cultivated over time.

Hopefully the research we covered on the growth mind-set in Chapter 1: Developing a Winning Outlook is still fresh in your mind. We *can* develop our skills so long as we have the right mental attitude and put in the work. We can *all* improve our flair for arguing and asserting ourselves more effectively.

Whatever your current level of ability – whether you want to improve on the questionnaire measure of Assertion or Respect For Others or both – you can do it with effort and patience. So go on, get started.

Onwards and upwards

- First of all, remember that it's fiendishly difficult to win an argument when emotions are high. Whenever possible, it's much better to have a calm, rational discussion when you (and others) can prepare your proposals and discuss what you each want from a situation.

- Use the questionnaire starting on page 40 to diagnose your current interpersonal style. The questionnaire teaches us that effective Responsible Assertiveness requires both Assertion and Respect For Others; one without the other is only half of the picture. Once you understand whether you need to work either on your Assertion skills or on your Respect For Others skills (or both), you can take the necessary steps to begin your improvement.

- Remember that either/or thinking (categorizing folks as either entirely one thing or wholly something else) is usually an unhelpful oversimplification. People are rarely angry, generous, uncooperative or anything else 100 per cent of the time. Keeping in mind the concept of both/and allows us to think about people and situations in a more realistic and therefore less combative way.

- Enhance your assertiveness by using the DEAR method to describe situations, express your opinions, acknowledge others' perspectives and recommend solutions. If Assertion is currently a challenge for you, putting the DEAR technique into action may at first feel awkward or unnerving. But it's a tried-and-tested approach that has helped many people to get their way more effectively.

- If bolstering your Respect For Others score is your goal, start with the twin techniques of perspective-giving (i.e. allowing people to tell you what they feel and want) and perspective-taking (i.e. summarizing and paraphrasing what they said). After all, while people repeatedly protest that colleagues, bosses, friends or even family "don't listen enough", you rarely hear the complaint that they "listen too much".

- Finally, bear in mind that becoming more effective at winning arguments is perhaps best conceived of as *pre-empting* quarrels and instead listening to others, showing that we comprehend their points of view, and then carefully sharing our ideas.

3

Winning the Pitch

**If history were taught in the form of stories,
it would never be forgotten.**
Rudyard Kipling

T wo true stories.

One. Several years ago, my partner and I brought home an eight-week-old Miniature Schnauzer puppy and named him Byron. With his oversized paws, floppy ears and doleful eyes peeking out from under little grey eyebrows, he was the definition of cute.

We took him to the vet for his first set of vaccinations and she warned us not to let him out of the house until he had built up his immunity. So we dutifully kept him inside for his first few weeks with us.

We noticed straightaway that our darling puppy urinated 20 times and did eight poos *in a single day*. Sometimes he would manage to relieve himself on some newspaper that we'd laid out. More often than not, though, we would find a little pool of urine or a couple of brown nuggets on our beautiful natural wooden floorboards. So yes, we were constantly mopping up behind him – pretty much every 20 minutes or so from the moment Byron woke up till he fell asleep at night.

Don't get me wrong: it's so rewarding to have him around now that he's fully house-trained. But he was so much work to begin with.

Two. Shortly after graduating from university – so I was in my mid-20s – I went for my first ever job interview. I wanted to work as a management consultant so I approached a recruitment firm that specialized in placing candidates into the management consultancy industry. Luckily, I had a strong academic track record and a little work experience so was offered a job interview with a small firm of consultants almost immediately.

I bought a suit, polished my shoes and went along for the interview. I felt confident that, with my scholastic success, I would easily impress the interviewer and land the job.

When I arrived for the interview, I was ushered into a small meeting room. A woman wearing a blood-red suit jacket with enormous shoulder pads introduced herself as Jeanette, one of the directors of the business. After exchanging pleasantries, she flashed me a shark-like grin and asked her first interview question: "So, I'm sure you know that we're a smaller consultancy with only a dozen consultants. Why would you wish to work for a small firm like us rather than one of the large, established consultancies like McKinsey or KPMG?"

Hmm. I thought about it for a moment but couldn't come up with an answer. I sheepishly told Jeanette that I didn't know. I simply hadn't done *any* preparation for the interview – it had never occurred to me that I would need to. Going into that interview, I had assumed that having a first-class honours degree and a doctorate in psychology would have any employer practically begging to hire me.

I was wrong, of course. Unsurprisingly, I didn't get offered the job.

So why am I telling you about a puppy and my bungled job interview?

Allowing people to come to their own conclusions

Imagine that I had started this chapter differently. Suppose that instead of the little anecdotes above, I had simply stated:

> *Don't get a dog unless you're ready to put in a lot of hard work.*

> *Don't go to a job interview unless you've done plenty of preparation about the company that's interviewing you.*

Would you have taken on board the messages? Probably not. They sound too trite – patronizingly obvious.

At a recent party, I mentioned to a glamorous 20-something woman that I had a dog. She ooh-ed and ahh-ed, waved her manicured hands around excitedly and said that she was desperate to get a dog. Chatting a little more, I discovered that she was a singleton with a full-time job and a flourishing social life; as such, she wasn't going to be able to look after a dog properly. Dogs are pack animals who crave human company; without it, they get anxious and destroy furniture, and sometimes end up getting given away because their owners can't cope.

I couldn't tell her outright: "You shouldn't get a dog. I don't think you'd be able to look after one properly." That would have come across as preachy and insulting and, worse still, she may not have listened to me anyway. But telling her a story – our experience, and the sheer messiness, of bringing our dog into our home – persuaded her not to get a dog.

I've shared the story of my botched job interview many times. I often get invited by university careers services to talk about how to land the perfect job. And I use my misadventure to highlight the importance of proper interview preparation. I use it to make the point that it doesn't matter how smart you are or how good your academic grades may be; you won't get the job if you don't know enough about the employer that is thinking about offering you a job.

There's a saying that facts tell, but stories sell. Telling my own story of bringing our dog Byron home changed that party-goer's mind. Telling roomfuls of university students about my silly blunder illustrates the need for adequate preparation so much more effectively than if I were simply to spell out the same message.

Stories are timeless and everywhere

Evolutionary psychologists believe that humans have been telling stories for tens of thousands of years. When our ancestors sought to amuse or entertain, they swapped anecdotes. They bragged about their achievements by turning them into epic poems. When they wanted to warn people against bad behaviour, they shared fables and parables. Take just about any culture anywhere in the world and you'll find examples of legends, myths and fairy tales that have been passed from generation to generation.[1]

It's no coincidence that most of the world's major religions convey their ideals not through dry lists of dos and don'ts but through stories. The Old Testament of the Christian bible, for example, consists of story after story. Hundreds of millions of folks worldwide – irrespective of their actual religious beliefs – know the stories of Adam and Eve, Noah's Ark, David and Goliath, Samson and Delilah and many others. In Buddhist scripture, the path to enlightenment is taught not through bullet points but by following the trials of Siddhartha Gautama, otherwise known as the Buddha.

It's a relatively recent phenomenon that modern-day people use facts and statistics to justify their arguments. Most adults from even a century ago probably didn't understand what percentages or ratios were, let alone how to use them to formulate a logical line of reasoning. Instead, if they wanted to warn others off from doing something bad or encourage them to behave in a certain way, they told stories.

But even today, people tell stories to sell their ideas, concepts and even themselves. Top salespeople, for example, know that the best way to tempt a customer is to tell graphic stories to illustrate how their products saved the day – or how someone who *didn't* use one of their offerings crashed and burned.

Top salespeople tell graphic stories to illustrate how their products saved the day.

Marketing brochures often contain case studies describing how individuals, families or whole organizations benefitted or succeeded as a result of using a product or service. And, when you strip it down to its core, what is a case study? Merely a more formal name for a story.

Now you may be thinking that *you* don't need to sell in your life. Maybe you don't sell products or services to customers or clients for a living. But I'd argue that every one of us needs to pitch ideas and sell daily.

Want a promotion? You need to sell your ideas and persuade people that your projects are the ones to back. Need to raise money for an animal shelter or for starving children? You have to sell your cause. Want to lobby the government or convert your neighbours into going green? Sell.

Even persuading someone to go on a date with you involves selling yourself as interesting, charming and sexy. Or if you want to entice your friends into going on a beach holiday rather than camping in the woods, of course you need to pitch the idea to them.

Think about the most engaging, entertaining individuals you know – both amongst your friends as well as your work circles. If you analyze what they say or do that makes them such compelling people to be around, I'm willing to bet that most of them tell funny or passionate or terrifying or self-deprecating stories.

Speeches and presentations almost always work better when they include personal anecdotes. An hour-long presentation of bullet points can feel like hell for an audience. But the moment audiences hear the beginning of a story, they perk up. They look up from their emails and text messages and want to hear what transpired. Sometimes, they get the gratification of predicting the outcome. Other times, they get surprised. Either way, the person telling the tale wins by keeping people switched on and attentive.

Away from work, the best wedding speeches I've ever heard always involve romantic, amusing or salacious stories about the bride or groom. At funerals, the most heartfelt eulogies have centred on recollections about the trials and triumphs of the dearly departed.

Stories are memorable. Stories are persuasive. Whether used in writing, videos, face-to-face conversations or conference presentations, stories can both change minds and influence behaviour. But don't just take my word for it that stories are penetrating ways to influence people. What does the scientific evidence tell us?

Stories are memorable. Stories are persuasive.

The science of storytelling

Here's a thought experiment for you. Imagine that a dangerous virus is affecting people all over the world. Let's call it the feline flu pandemic. The virus causes a range of unpleasant symptoms and can be fatal in some cases but, thankfully, scientists have already concocted a vaccine which is 96 per cent effective.

Doctors want to encourage people of all ages to get vaccinated but they're not sure exactly how to persuade people to do so. They only have a limited advertising budget. Should they put out a fact-based press release or tell the story of a single sufferer?

This is precisely the question that Dutch researchers led by John de Wit at Utrecht University tried to answer. Let's continue our imaginary journey and suppose that you come across two newspaper cuttings talking about the importance of getting vaccinated. Which one of the following do you think is the more powerful and persuasive?

Every winter, tens of thousands of people around the country get the flu. However, a new, stronger so-called feline flu strain has reached the United Kingdom. Feline flu is estimated to have affected between 20,000 and 40,000 individuals in the UK since the beginning of the year. The age range of those who have contracted the virus range from very young children to the elderly. Both men and women are equally likely to be affected.

Typical symptoms include: a high temperature and sweating, a feeling of generalized feebleness, severe aches and pains in both muscles (particularly in the abdomen) and joints around the body, a headache and a sore throat. There may also be a loss of appetite and the sensation of "chills". In many cases, symptoms may also include diarrhoea and/or vomiting. In rare cases, individuals have also reported intense dizziness and seeing flashes of light in their eyes.

The acute symptoms tend to pass within 5 to 8 days. However, symptoms of infirmity may persist for several weeks thereafter. Approximately 13 in 100 patients may require treatment in hospital, for example for dehydration from diarrhoea. People with emphysema or other respiratory conditions may be at greater risk. The virus has also proved fatal in some cases. While the common winter flu tends to generate fatalities in people with existing medical conditions or those with compromised immune systems (e.g. the elderly), it seems that the feline flu is associated with an acute risk of death across all ages.

The vaccine is 96 per cent effective and is administered for free by your doctor. It is recommended that everyone should visit their doctor as soon as possible to receive the vaccination against feline flu.

Or here's a second version:

My name is Ashley and I'm a healthy 39-year-old. I go to the gym maybe twice a week (as much as my work as a financial analyst allows) and eat healthily, apart from having too many cakes. I get the occasional cold but don't often get ill.

In January, I remember feeling particularly tired one Sunday after-noon. By the evening, I was feeling extremely cold. I was shivering despite having brought a blanket into the lounge from upstairs. Sud-denly, I felt my stomach turning and I was sick. I couldn't get to the bathroom in time and I vomited onto my blanket and clothes.

I threw up again a couple more times that evening and I didn't sleep much that night. I was shivering because I felt so cold but at the same time my duvet was soaked with sweat. I couldn't go to work for the entire week. Even by Friday I was still feeling shaky and tired and a little out of breath even walking up the stairs to the bathroom.

I went back to work the following week but I got tired out quite quickly during the day and was exhausted by the evenings. It took me another two weeks before I had the energy to go back to the gym.

The vaccine is 96 per cent effective and is free from your doctor. If someone had told me that I could have avoided all of that vomit-ing, sweating, shaking and feeling awful for a whole week, I would gladly have paid a doctor £500 not to suffer any of that. So I recom-mend that you visit your doctor as soon as possible to receive the vaccination against the feline flu.

Both paragraphs are 284 words in length. But which one did you think was the more hard-hitting and convincing?

If you're like most people, you probably found the second account more graphic, evocative and persuasive. And that's precisely what de Wit and his team found too. People who read first-person testi-monials about their experience of living with disease were signifi-cantly more likely to get vaccinated than those who read impersonal facts and statistics about the disease.[2]

Stories didn't just persuade people. They saved lives.

If we're keeping score, that makes it: Stories 1, Statistics 0.

Understanding the irrational appeal of stories

Perhaps you're thinking that you or the crowd in your life are much more rational and prefer hard facts over unproven anecdotes. And yes, most people *think* that they're pretty rational and aren't influenced by trivial stories, but research tells us otherwise.

Most people *think* that they're pretty rational and aren't influenced by trivial stories, but research tells us otherwise.

Time for another piece of research. To illustrate this next study, let's contemplate a hypothetical scenario. An elderly aunt of yours – one of your favourite relatives – lives alone in the city and she's worried about her safety. She doesn't have a computer so asks you to go online to research a home security system for her.

You discover from a speedy Google search that there are two main manufacturers of alarm systems, Diamond Protection and Bulldog Guardian. Even though there are other retailers, they actually sell products made by one of these two big companies.

You also come across an article written in a highly respected consumer magazine saying that Diamond Protection's alarms are far superior to those of Bulldog Guardian. In laboratory tests, Diamond Protection outperformed Bulldog Guardian on just about every criterion. The scientists also surveyed several thousand homeowners with security systems made by either company and found that Bulldog Guardian's alarms broke down three times more frequently and were more costly to maintain. So the article is eminently clear: Diamond Protection's alarm systems are much, much better than those of Bulldog Guardian.

However, your Google search throws up a couple of surprising online complaints about Diamond Protection too. One is a blog post written by a young pair of newlyweds with the rather twee names Avery and Alice who installed Diamond Protection's system in their new home. When they went on holiday only three months later, their home was ransacked by intruders, who broke in through a rear window and stole pretty much everything they owned. The Diamond Protection alarm didn't go off until the couple returned home from holiday and put their key in the door!

Another online article reports that a man – a construction foreman called Connor – installed a Diamond Protection system, but the alarm kept going off in the night without good reason. He asked an engineer to come fix it but even after two visits the system still kept registering false alarms. Eventually, Connor decided to buy a Bulldog Guardian system. He threw the Diamond Protection system in the bin. OK, so you found the article on a tawdry gossip website known more for its semi-slanderous reportage of C-List celebrities. But the article wouldn't be a lie, would it?

So you have two sources of information to help you make a decision. One is the article focusing on lab tests and a survey saying that Diamond Protection beats Bulldog Guardian in nearly every way. The other is a couple of online articles written by people whose credentials you have no idea about. Given the choice, which of the two systems would you recommend for your beloved elderly aunt?

When I pose this question to groups of delegates during training sessions and workshops, probably around 80 to 90 per cent of people say that they would recommend Diamond Protection. After all, that's the logical, rational choice. That's what the scientists recommend, right?

Surely very few individuals would recommend something based only on a couple of unproven stories. Indeed, when research psychologists posed a similar choice to experimental participants, they found that 97 per cent of people said that they would recommend for another person the product endorsed by the independent consumer article rather than the flimsier anecdotal reports.

Rather sneakily, though, the researchers then gave participants the opportunity to take home one of the two products to try for themselves. And when it came to choosing something to use *for themselves*, 31 per cent of people changed their minds.[3]

That's like 97 per cent of folks saying that they would recommend the Diamond Protection system for their aunt – because they know it's the rational, sensible thing to do. They realize that they *should* recommend things predicated on evidence and facts. But then 31 per cent of people decide that what's good enough for that dear old aunt may not be good enough for them. The unproven stories ultimately won over one in three people – they couldn't help but be swayed, against their better judgement, by stories over facts.

Now, that scenario asks you to throw your support behind either a set of facts *or* a story. And the story won out for one in three people. So just imagine if you were trying to persuade people and had not only facts *but also* a story. Consider how powerful and persuasive that combination could be.

What is a story?

A well-told story somehow bypasses our defences to strike deep within our brains. But try to pin down exactly what a story is and you may find it harder than it may at first seem. After all, stories can be moving or merely instructive, tragic or uplifting, brutal or hilarious. They can surprise us or affirm what we believed all along.

A well-told story somehow bypasses our defences to strike deep within our brains.

Stories can be fictional exploits or retellings of real events. They can be set in the distant past, just a day ago or in a hypothetical future. They can be shared with one person in an intimate setting or with many people at the same time.

Cut to the core of a story, though, and what we discover is that all such adventures have characters or protagonists that either do something or to whom something happens. There may only be one protagonist or there may be a cast of many.

In J. K. Rowling's bestselling series of books, for example, we get introduced to Harry Potter. We learn that he's an orphan and that he lives in a cupboard under the stairs with a family who tell him he's no good.

Or take the original *Star Wars* movie, which has more of an ensemble of characters. We first meet Princess Leia, a resistance fighter seeking to defeat a tyrannical galactic empire. Seemingly by chance, we then become acquainted with a young farmer called Luke Skywalker, who recruits the roguish Han Solo to help rescue the princess.

In the New Testament, we learn that Jesus Christ was born to humble beginnings in the town of Bethlehem to Joseph and his betrothed Mary. But then he hears a voice from Heaven addressing him and telling him that he is the Son of God.

The protagonists usually encounter an event or series of events. Each may present an obstacle, conflict or crisis. Depending on what happens, we may learn that the protagonists are plucky heroes who struggle on through or are perhaps ill-fated victims who fail in spite of their best efforts.

Harry Potter discovers that he's a wizard and gets taken to the magical school of Hogwarts. He has to fend off some bullying kids while also fighting all manner of creatures and evil witches and wizards.

Luke Skywalker conquers his own fears and learns a new skill – becoming a Jedi – in order to rescue the princess and overthrow Darth Vader. Han Solo overcomes his personal greed and, in doing so, discovers that he wants to fight the forces of evil too.

Jesus feels compelled to preach the word of God, which he does by giving sermons and by telling parables. However, his actions stir up ill-feeling among the Romans, who govern the lands, as well as the existing religious rulers, who doubt that he is the Son of God.

And finally we reach the end, in which we find out how the situation resolved itself. Maybe the protagonists overcame the obstacles and resolved the crisis. Or they may be beaten down by it.

So Harry Potter vanquishes the evil wizard Voldemort. Luke Skywalker, Han Solo and Princess Leia destroy the Death Star and send Darth Vader spinning into space. Jesus is crucified but rises from the dead, proving to his doubters that he really was the Son of God.

Actually, the protagonists of a story don't even need to be people. I was at a fund-raising event recently for the renovation of a celebrated old theatre in London, and the speaker told the tale of how the building had survived two world wars but had fallen into disrepair in recent years. Listening to the travails and ordeals that the grand old building had suffered made for as absorbing a story as any good book. So there's no reason why the protagonist of a story couldn't be a product, an animal, a location – pretty much anything, perhaps?

But the point is this: whether fiction or fact, most stories follow a similar pattern. And here's the good news. You don't have to be a master troubadour or a modern-day bard, because we can *all* exploit this simple pattern to tell effective stories.

Studying stories

This chapter is all about effective storytelling. And we shall shortly cover a simple framework for telling effective stories. But a good start is to become more analytical as you read, listen to and watch other stories.

How are your favourite novels or biographies structured? What makes a story in the news compelling? What in particular makes the plot of a film or TV show engaging?

Becoming more critical as you come across stories will help you to identify the elements that will help you to inject greater interest into your stories.

"SOAR vividly"

Over the years I've trained many people in the art of telling effective stories. I've worked with groups of job hunters ranging from seasoned executives to lowly graduates who needed to sell themselves more effectively during job interviews. I've worked with management consultants, engineers, lawyers, accountants and salespeople across all sorts of industries who wanted to pitch their services to their clients and customers.

I contend that all you need to do is "SOAR vividly". I'll discuss the four letters of the SOAR acronym first and come back to the "vividly" part in the next section.

SOAR stands for:

- **Situation.** So what's the background to the story that you wish to tell? Who are the protagonists or characters in your case study or anecdote? And what do you need to tell your audience in order to grab their attention and make them want to listen to the rest?

- **Obstacles.** The most effective stories involve protagonist(s) who battle to overcome obstacles. These could be physical problems, such as a lack of resources, or actual opponents; these could also be personal challenges, such as having to overcome one's fears, doubts or base human nature. But obstacles are essential. Researchers at Harvard University have documented something called the "Underdog Effect": audiences like and warm to protagonists who overcome arduous difficulties as opposed to protagonists who have every advantage to begin with.[4] Audiences want to know what the protagonist(s) had to contend with. So what are the setbacks or barriers your protagonists faced?

- **Actions.** Once you've introduced the obstacles, your audience wants to know what the protagonists did to deal with each hurdle. If you're telling an epic about yourself, what steps did "I" or "we" take to tackle each obstacle? Or if you're recounting an anecdote about someone else, what did "he" or "she" or "they" do? If something didn't work, what did the protagonist(s) do next?

- **Resolution (and Revelation).** Finally, there's the end to the story. Audiences don't like to be left hanging. Did the protagonist(s) achieve success or failure? Was there any bizarre twist in the tale that the audience may not have expected? What did the protagonist(s) learn? And, by extension, what's the lesson, message or emotion-laden warning that you're trying to sneak past your audience's defences?

Beginning to SOAR

Your turn. Have a go. What stories could you tell to spread your ideas or lessons?

Perhaps you run a charity and want to promote a philanthropic cause. Maybe you're an entrepreneur who needs investors to dip into their pockets to fund your latest venture. Or you may be a manager, a supplier, even a parent who wants to change the attitudes or behaviour of your employees, your customers or your kids.

Write the words Situation, Obstacles, Actions and Resolution/Revelation down the side of a sheet of paper. Even better, open up your computer and create a table in a document.

Then under each heading have a go at scripting what the background was, the obstacles the protagonist(s) faced, the actions the protagonist(s) took and what was ultimately achieved.

You could tell a story drawn from real life featuring you as the protagonist. Or you could tell a tale about colleagues, family or friends that you've witnessed. To convince customers to buy from you, share stories – effectively testimonials – about the challenges that other customers faced and how you, your products or services helped them.

Or your story could be fictitious. Asking audiences to pretend that they are experiencing an imaginary but realistic situation can sometimes be just as effective.

As we progress through this chapter, I'll give you more advice on how to turn the skeleton of your story into a stronger one.

Your aim is to supply just enough detail to paint a picture for your audience so that they can see it in their imaginations. Help your audience to feel as if it's a movie playing out right in front of them.

Say you're trying to explain to customers how they could benefit from what you did for another customer. Perhaps your story could play to their hopes or ambitions of what they could reap too.

Or suppose you're seeking to warn a group of youths about the dangers of drugs or drink driving. Maybe you could try shocking or disgusting them to warn them off forever.

Think in particular about the emotions you wish to spark in your audience. Do you want them to fear the consequences of not taking action? Do you need them to pity the plight of the protagonist in your story and reach for their wallets? Or do you want to enthuse and excite people about the benefits of behaving differently? Whatever your goal, the key to galvanizing your audience into action is to make them *feel* something.

> The key to galvanizing your audience into action is to make them *feel* something.

I'm not saying that the SOAR acronym can transform anyone into a miraculous storyteller – the kind of person who can stride on stage and enrapture vast, thronging audiences for hours at a time. But it can help us to pull together effective narratives to tell people about our concepts, ideas, products or even our own achievements.

I once coached a religious, abstemious but financially savvy man in his mid-30s who worked at an investment bank. I'll call him Leo. He felt that he was being held back from promotion despite the fact that he had brokered as many deals as some of his colleagues who had been promoted above him. His bosses told him that he wasn't enough of a team player – which he took to mean that he didn't hang around enough with his colleagues drinking in bars and that he was too quiet. He didn't engage in enough banter and talk up his own achievements in the brash, self-congratulatory fashion that his more bullish counterparts did.

But after I shared with him the SOAR acronym, he made a concerted effort to tell his colleagues what he had been up to. Rather than having to think up artificial ways to boast about his successes, Leo found it easier to tell carefully crafted – but seemingly spontaneous – stories about the lessons he hit upon in his work.

He started by setting out the challenges he faced, for example clients saying "no" because they didn't have the budget or because they already had relationships with other investment banks. Then he told his colleagues how he took every obstacle, every objection and problem and acted to deal with them. And, of course, the resolution usually finished with the happy ending of how he landed a new client or, less frequently, the crucial lesson he learnt from a less joyful conclusion.

I only worked with Leo for a few months and we worked on other skills too, but it seemed that planned storytelling helped him considerably by allowing him to talk about his achievements in a non-boastful manner. A little over a year later I received a card and a bottle of champagne from him telling me that he had been promoted.

Using vivid language

When I'm running leadership development programmes for client organizations and covering the topic of emotional intelligence, I often recount the true story of how the chief executive of a marketing consultancy, whom I'll call Martin, effectively destroyed his own business.

A bit of background. Martin was an intellectually brilliant academic who had founded his own business in the late 1990s. He had degrees from both Oxford and Harvard universities. And his intellectual prowess made him dazzling to work with.

Now in his late 50s, he had thick eyebrows and a shock of overly black hair, which many amongst his team believed to be dyed. With a tall but moderately overweight build, Martin had a booming voice and a perpetually sweaty forehead. He talked loudly. He laughed loudly. And when he was in a good mood, he was inspiring and fun to be around.

But when he was in a bad mood, his team of consultants really suffered. He banged his fist on the table during meetings when his team reported bad news. He made threats about people's jobs when they fell short of their targets. He mocked his employees in a joking-but-not-joking manner, rolled his eyes, and sometimes walked out of meetings in visible despair.

When the economy tanked and the company's problems piled up, he finally lost his temper one time too many. He made threats during a team meeting which weren't just mildly troubling but outright offensive.

The result? Three of his most senior executives decided that they had had enough. They were experienced people but Martin treated them more like inadequate children. They managed to skirt around the usual non-compete clauses and legal protections that Martin had put in place to set up their own businesses: one left to set up on her own while the other two banded together to set up another rival business. Over the course of less than nine months, the three departing executives took more than half of Martin's clients with them.

Poor Martin. He was a hard-working and talented executive in many ways. But regrettably his inability to control his rage – his lack of emotional intelligence about his impact on others – was his undoing.

The end.

In reading that story, did you notice anything unnecessary in its retelling?

Read it again and you'll see that I took a few sentences to describe Martin. I told you his approximate age and what he looked like. I told you about his physical size and how he had a propensity to perspire. Maybe you imagined him as someone with a paunch or just someone with a larger-than-average build. Also, you learnt that he was loud.

Strictly speaking, none of those details should matter. I could have saved several sentences by jumping to the fact that he often experienced dark moods.

But, actually, studies tell us that those apparently unimportant details *do* matter.

The science of the small stuff

Research conducted by psychologists Melanie Green and Timothy Brock at Ohio State University tells us that people are more likely to be persuaded by a story when they feel "transported" by it. When individuals feel "transported", they feel immersed in the characters, detail and narrative; they become so intent on following the narrative and finding out what happened that they may even become less aware of the real world around them.[4]

The research reminded me of a time recently when I met a friend of mine outside a train station. I was running late and saw that she was already there, standing outside the entrance reading a book – *The Hunger Games*, in fact. When I went up to her and said hello, I made her jump! She literally jolted upright and cried, "Oh!" She was so engrossed in the story – she had been so transported – that she had lost track of what was going on around her.

The more we can paint an immersive mental picture for an audience, the more likely we will be to transport them and therefore win them over. Whether we are dreaming up a hypothetical scenario or telling a story about a real situation, we would be wise to depict a graphic and involving scene for people – something so intense that they almost feel it's happening to them.

That's why lawyers in court cases often go to fantastic lengths to paint vivid mental images. They know that, when seeking to establish the guilt (or innocence) of a defendant in the eyes of a judge and jury, the details matter.

For example, a lawyer in a grisly shooting incident could say: "On the night of January 11th, Edgar Broughton was shot by an intruder in his home." Very straightforward and factual.

But it would be more advantageous to begin with something like: "It's January 11th, just after midnight. It's a cold clear night and the moon is almost full. Picture a quiet suburban street and the home of one Edgar Broughton. The house has a white wooden porch with a neat, emerald-green lawn and a row of pale-pink roses out front. And it was here, in his very own home, that Edgar Broughton was tragically gunned down by an intruder."

Success at persuading people through purely factual argument hinges on convincing audiences that you are both a credible source and have good intentions. In contrast, the research duo Green and Brock suggest that stories "might be used to advantage by low-credible sources or by speakers who lack cogent arguments".

In other words, audiences that feel transported by an absorbing story may not pay attention to whether the source is credible or not. They get swept away by the narrative.

So, the more we can transport people away into our stories and help them to visualize what happened, the more persuasive our narratives become. That's why I use the phrase "SOAR vividly" as an aide-memoire for individuals who want to tell more effective stories. The "vividly" bit turns out to be rather essential when it comes to giving birth to stories that truly come alive in the minds of an audience.

The more we can paint an immersive mental picture for an audience, the more likely we will be to win them over.

So add in those finer points. Sometimes more words can lead to greater persuasion. Even if your audience doesn't quite know why you've added those vivid details into your story, *you* will know that you are transporting them to exactly where you want them to be.

Introducing vividness

Over to you again. Hopefully you have started to assemble the components of a story – the situation, obstacles, actions and resolution – as you'll get the most out of this chapter if you have the bare bones of one. Now have a go at adding in a vivid detail or two now.

You could include a colourful phrase or two about the protagonist(s) in your tale. What outstanding physical characteristics did they have? Were they wearing anything unusual? Did they have any particular mannerisms – speech, posture, movement?

Perhaps you could set the scene by describing the locale of your meeting, such as a particularly messy office, a lavish restaurant, a bumpy taxi, whatever. Maybe mention the time of year – for example that the incident took place in the heat of June when the air conditioning was broken and tempers were fraying.

What one or two phrases of vivid detail will you use to pull your listeners or readers deeper into your adventure?

Making money through stories

Storytelling is like a Trojan Horse that allows us to sneak our pitches through audiences' defences. Whether real or imaginary, stories seem to swerve around people's natural scepticism to find their target at some intensely profound level.

It should hardly surprise you then that more and more organizations are realizing the power of storytelling as a tool for winning hearts and changing minds. In a recent fund-raising campaign, for example, the American Red Cross sent video cameras to 300 individuals and asked them to capture their tales of how they had each been helped by the charity. The YouTube trailer for the campaign is only 1 minute and 58 seconds long, but I dare you to watch it without feeling a real tug on your emotions – I felt my eyes welling up with tears less than 30 seconds into the video! (I'll put a link to their campaign in the notes at the back of the book.[5])

Linda Honan, the creative executive at advertising agency BBDO New York, who headed up the campaign, explained: "Every time we started to talk about an ad campaign, we worried that it felt a little contrived or boastful."

Instead, she and her team took the route of asking individuals to share their own, very personal experiences of how the American Red Cross had either saved their lives or helped them to save the life of someone else: "We found the purest way to push the story [of the American Red Cross] out was to have the people whose lives have been touched tell their story."

Regardless of the purity of the approach, science informs us that stories are far more effective at getting people to part with cash. In one notable study, researchers recruited people to read either some factual information about starvation in Africa or the story of a single, starving African girl. Those who read the descriptive passage donated on average $1.21. Those who read about the starving girl named Rokia donated $2.12 – an increase of a whopping 76 per cent more money.[6]

Imagine if you could boost the success of *your* sales pitches by 76 per cent. You'd be more than a little pleased, right?

Focusing on the O and A

I'm not saying that all stories follow the SOAR pattern. Some authors start with the situation or resolution first and then go back to cover the obstacles or actions. The four elements are still there, but perhaps tumbled into a different order, such as SROA or RSOA.

For example, when we read the biographies of famous people, we often already know what they achieved. Whether we're reading about a business leader or a celebrated actor, we know where they've got to – what the resolution to the tale is. What intrigues us is *how* they got there – the obstacles they encountered and the actions they took to get to the top.

Pick up the biography of Virgin entrepreneur Richard Branson or GE chief executive Jack Welch and you'll read how they succeeded in spite of a lack resources and how they outmanoeuvred sluggish competitors. Read about actors or entertainers and you'll uncover how they overcame poverty, tragic family circumstances, unsupportive teachers or even abuse.

What makes stories gripping are the descriptions of the obstacles people encountered and the plucky actions they took along the way. And that's why in this next box I recommend distinguishing between the distinct obstacles you faced. So when you're pitching your wares or yourself, be sure to make the obstacles you faced – along with the actions you took – stand out. Here's a further set of pointers for honing the stories you tell.

> What makes stories gripping are the descriptions of the obstacles people encountered and the plucky actions they took along the way.

Taking "SOAR vividly" to the next level

Storytelling is as much art as science. And I would be lying if I said that I could give you an ironclad set of rules that would enable you to craft powerful, persuasive stories without fail. Often, the best way to get better at telling stories is to test drive some stories, see how they work and hone them over time. However, here are some further pointers that may help you out:

- **Situation**: spend only a little time laying out the background or set-up to your story. If you read classic fiction – for example a *Sherlock Holmes* story or anything by Charles Dickens or Emily Brontë – you'll notice there's a lot of

(Continued)

background description and relatively little action. But modern 21st-century fiction concentrates much more on the action because folks in the pacey digital age get bored so easily. So be careful not to supply too much background information. How will you capture your audience's attention or arouse their curiosity as quickly as possible?

- **Obstacle 1 + Actions**: don't just list all of the obstacles that you or the protagonist(s) faced straightaway. Begin by talking about the first hitch or dilemma and the actions that the protagonist(s) took to overcome it. Was it successful?

- **Obstacle 2 + Actions**: next, move on to the next difficulty or challenge. What was it? And what did the protagonist(s) to do deal with this one?

- **Obstacle 3 + Actions**: and then repeat as often as you like until you reach the end of your story. Bear in mind that if you're giving an hour-long presentation, you may be able to talk at length about multiple obstacles in your saga. But if you want a quick anecdote, then fewer or even just one obstacle may be enough to make the point.

- **Resolution**: finally, talk about the result, what transpired, the impact on the protagonist(s). Did good things happen, suggesting that our audience should emulate the protagonist(s)? Or did things turn out badly, meaning that we should steer clear of what the perpetrator(s) did? If you're trying to hit your audience with an emotion – if you're trying to make them laugh, cry, gasp or groan – this is when you do it.

- **Vividly**: remember to add in those vivid details so that you're not just describing what happened but also where it happened, what the characters looked like and how it felt. Remember that it can be the seemingly irrelevant titbits of detail that allow a listener to visualize a story and feel truly immersed in it.

Adding in a little TLC

TLC customarily stands for tender loving care. But in the context of pitching stories that change minds and behaviour, TLC stands for time, location and characters.

It's not always a must-have to add in time and location, and you can leave them out if you're very short of time. But even a single sentence or two may be enough to provide a clearer image for your audience that helps them to picture the scene more vividly.

Think about how we start stories for children. The quintessential start for a fairy tale is to say something like: "A long time ago in a magical kingdom far, far away. . ." In other words, we include a time and location before introducing the characters: TLC.

If you're struggling to set the scene for your story, here are some further pointers:

- **Time.** You can be as vague or precise as you like about when your story took place. For example, something like "When Elena was a girl growing up" implies that the story is set in the past or that we may encounter Elena as an adult. But it doesn't specifically mention a date or even a decade. Contrast that to openers such as "Back in the 1980s, I remember when . . ." or "You won't believe what happened to me last week. It was lunchtime – just past 1 o'clock on a Thursday – and I was . . ." Usually, just a sentence is enough about the timing of the story as audiences want to get to what actually happened.

- **Location.** As with time, you can be fairly general or ultra-specific about where your action took place. Contrast "When Elena was a girl growing up in Russia" (which specifies a country) versus "I was walking down Station Street and had crossed the road opposite the Burger King" (which is much more specific). Again, a single sentence may be enough to describe where the story took place.

- **Characters.** You may not have to provide much (or even any) background if you're telling a story about yourself – especially if you're standing in front of an audience! But if you're talking about multiple protagonists, it may be worth thinking about how you will introduce each hero or victim. For example, if I'm sharing an anecdote about one of my clients, Ingrid, and how she eventually got promoted above her boss, Chris, I may need to offer a little description of both Ingrid and Chris.

Suppose you're writing a case study that has to be fewer than 300 words long. Or you're preparing some anecdotes to use briefly during a 30-minute sales meeting with a potential customer. In these cases, you may not have the luxury of mentioning the time, location and characters. But even so, it's worth having them in mind. Knowing *when* and *where* a story took place and *who* was involved will help you to paint a more vivid picture of what happened.

Matching backgrounds

One reason I'm so keen on wading through research studies is that it helps to take the guesswork out of life. And one pioneering study in particular allows us to turn storytelling from an art form into more of a science.

Shortly before a US presidential election, researchers Geoff Kaufman and Lisa Libby invited a class of undergraduate students at Ohio State University to take part in a rather elegant experiment.

They asked the participants to read a fictitious student's first-person narrative (i.e. a story told from the student's own perspective:

"I did this, I did that . . ."). The student wanted to vote in an election and overcame several obstacles – car problems, rain and long lines at the polling booth – in order to do so.

But here's the twist. The researchers secretly split the participants into two groups and gave each group a slightly altered version of the story to read. One version of the account mentioned that the protagonist was a student at Ohio State University. The other version revealed that the protagonist was a student at Denison University, another university in the same state. Otherwise, though, the two narratives were identical.

A week later, the researchers emailed the participants to find out whether they had actually voted or not in the real-world presidential election.

The result? Twenty-nine per cent of those who had read about a student at rival Denison University said they had voted. But a staggering 65 per cent of those who read about the student at Ohio State University ended up voting.[7]

Psychologists use the terms "ingroup" and "outgroup" to refer to people we identify with versus people we don't identify with. Participants who believed that the story was about someone from the same university – the same ingroup – were more than twice as likely to vote as those who read about someone from the different university, or outgroup.

Hopefully the implication of the study is clear enough. Were we trying to alter people's behaviour through a story, we would be wise to speak about someone who had a similar background to the audience – someone from the ingroup rather than an outgroup.

We would be wise to speak about someone who had a similar background to the audience.

Matching stories to audiences

We all have favourite anecdotes or stories that we like to tell. But how useful are yours for actually influencing and persuading your target audiences?

If you are preparing a speech for an audience of mainly Asian women, then picking an Asian woman protagonist for any stories you tell makes sense. Or at least pick a protagonist who is either Asian or a woman. Or if you're shooting a video primarily for finance directors of medium-sized businesses – well, I'm sure you can guess who your stories should ideally feature!

Think for a moment about the stories you'd like to tell. Will the protagonist(s) within them *genuinely resonate* with your audience?

Turning molehills back into mountains

There's an old English adage that goes, "Don't make a mountain out of a molehill." It means that we shouldn't blow things out of proportion. And as far as advice for life goes, it's a splendid idea. We mostly shouldn't treat relatively small incidents as if they were crises. We should let the minor missteps and transgressions go rather than allowing them to assume too great a role in our lives.

But when it comes to telling persuasive stories, it may often help us to do the precise opposite: to turn molehills back into mountains.

The principle reminds me of a time I coached an executive in the pharmaceuticals industry, called Karolina, who was struggling to land a new job. An effervescent Hungarian woman in her mid-40s who spoke with the urgency of the over-caffeinated, she had a superb track record and had been invited to numerous interviews but wasn't getting any offers. So I met her and put her through a mock interview to see what she was doing wrong.

She spoke with confidence and the élan of the well-travelled. However, I spotted that she was downplaying her accomplishments despite the fact that she was far from shy. She wasn't making light of her skills out of bashfulness or modesty but seemingly because her thoughts were bubbling out of her without enough structure.

Whenever I asked her to give me examples of her achievements – for instance with questions like "Tell me about a time you coached a struggling member of your team" – she skipped over the details. She spent far too much time setting up the scenario and rambling on about the background to the situation. She talked only briefly about the obstacles she faced and actions she took. Case in point: she said that she had coached one of her team members who experienced some "personal upheaval" in his life. Then she jumped to the conclusion, the resolution of the story.

At first, her story didn't sound that impressive. But when I questioned her in depth, I discovered that the member of her team had suffered a bereavement – the death of his brother – which had precipitated childcare issues at home, a period of understandably terrible personal unhappiness and a drop in productivity at work.

It was only when we explored what those problems were – by getting into enough detail to turn those molehills back into mountains – that I discovered the lengths to which she had gone in order to support her team member. A less interested interviewer might not have asked for the same amount of detail and so Karolina would have lost the opportunity to showcase her skills.

So have a think when you're trying to pitch something to your audience. Say you're pitching your company's services to a potential client by telling the story of how you helped a previous client, ABC Technology. You could start by describing ABC Technology's situation and need. You could describe the actions your company took and the result that ABC Technology got. But it would be a fairly humdrum, uninspiring story. It wouldn't present your audience with anything to make them sit up and want to listen to the story.

But imagine talking about ABC Technology's problems. Perhaps you quoted that the project would take three months and signed a contract to that effect. But then you uncovered further problems which led you to the horrific conclusion that it would actually take you six months . . .

In telling this new version of the story, pause for a moment. Stop. Let the statement hang in the air. And imagine what could be going through your potential client's mind. Clearly, your audience would want to know: how did you solve the problem? How did you cram six months' worth of work into a mere three months?

By pointing out the obstacles that you or the protagonist(s) in your story encountered, you create a sense of jeopardy, a feeling of suspense. You automatically raise questions in the minds of your audience. You make them wonder: "What happened next?"

People are curious by nature. Present them with a mystery and they can't help but want to understand *what happened next.*

And that's the perfect moment to strike. To explain how you or the protagonist(s) saved the day, the actions that were taken and the resolution that was achieved.

When I'm running training sessions on storytelling and making effective pitches in business, some clients struggle to take it all in.

Other clients think that all of it sounds really straightforward and obvious. So the theory can appear confusing for some but too simplistic for others. Irrespective of their concerns, I say the same thing to both of these groups: it's only when you try to *apply* the framework to your own experiences that it will start to make sense and truly come alive.

To construct their own "SOAR vividly" stories, many clients find it useful to draw up and then fill in a table as follows:

Time	
Location	
(Ingroup) Character(s)	
Situation	
(Mountainous) Obstacle 1	
Actions	
(Mountainous) Obstacle 2	
Actions	
(Mountainous) Obstacle 3	
Actions	
Resolution (and Revelation)	
Vivid details	

Let's have a go at filling in the table.

We begin with the TLC of your story: time, location, characters. *When* did it happen? *Where* did it happen? And *who* was involved? We may not need to mention these in our final story, but it will help us to construct the rest of the story if we at least have these details in mind. I include the word "ingroup" in brackets to remind us that we should – as far as possible – pick a character, a protagonist, who matches the audience.

Then we think about how we'll introduce the situation. How much background is enough, but not too heavy going or boring?

Next, we consider the obstacles that the protagonist(s) encountered: each problem, issue or challenge. But we need to remember to turn those molehills back into mountains by including enough dramatic detail. We want to make these obstacles seem sufficiently momentous so that our protagonist(s)'s actions and ultimate success can appear all the more heroic – or their downfall even more tragic.

But eventually you always end with the resolution and its implied revelation for your audience. Did the protagonist(s) succeed or at least learn and grow? Or did the protagonist(s) fail and, in flunking out, teach us lessons about how *not* to behave?

Running your story through a final check

Stories can allow us to pitch our ideas, products or services (or even ourselves) whether in person, via Skype or in print. But a truly persuasive story should be more than just a factual description of what occurred. Report only the facts and it becomes a dull transcript – more like the kind of description someone would write when making an insurance claim – rather than an engaging, evocative adventure. A storyteller should be able to make an audience *want* to find out what came off next.

Imagine watching a TV detective show where you really don't care who murdered the victim. Imagine watching a play at the theatre and being more interested in checking your Facebook updates or Twitter feed. Or how it feels when you're reading a school textbook rather than a gripping novel that makes you want to turn page after page to read more, more, more.

Sometimes the storytellers that I've worked with get caught up in working out *what* happened, *when* it happened, *where* it happened and so on. But the ultimate test for your story is: do people *want* to listen to your story and its outcome?

Stand-up comedians seem like gifted, master storytellers. But even the very best have to prepare and hone their stories. Many comedians practise their craft at dozens of small gigs before they decide on the anecdotes that will work best on television or on the arena tour. So don't expect to write a perfect story in a single sitting.

If you're putting together a script for an important meeting – say to investors, shareholders, potential clients or even an interview panel – I'd suggest drafting your stories and then setting them to one side. After a few days, come back to them. Read them out aloud and ask yourself: do *you* think it's a great story?

This final box may help you to refine your stories and will hopefully propel you towards more persuasive stories.

> The ultimate test for your story is: do people *want* to listen to your story and its outcome?

Ensuring your stories transport people

The Ohio State University researchers Melanie Green and Timothy Brock devised a scale for measuring the degree of transportation. If you want to make sure that your stories are sufficiently engaging to whisk your audience away (and

(Continued)

therefore change their attitudes or behaviours), you may wish to use the following checklist.

Share your story with a couple of friends or colleagues and ask them:

- When reading (or listening to) the story, could you picture the exploits described in it?
- Were you mentally involved in the story while reading (or listening) to it?
- Did you have a vivid image of the protagonist(s) in the story?
- Did you want to learn how the story ended?
- Did the story affect you emotionally?

Of course, not every story will elicit a "yes" response to all of these questions. We may not always have time to tell lengthy sagas that fully transport people. Or sometimes, we may wish to tell only shorter anecdotes that serve a simpler purpose. But the very best stories will get a resounding "yes" to all five.

Like most skills, storytelling doesn't come overnight. But it doesn't take much practice either.

I worked with a manager who had been told that his presentations were effective but somewhat lacklustre. Anthony, a dark-bearded Scotsman with a disarming Edinburgh accent, was at first puzzled by the remarks. He knew that he was articulate and poised when giving presentations; he made good eye contact with audiences and spoke in a clear, ringing voice. But with a little digging, we gleaned the truth.

His colleagues saw him as someone who could get an audience nodding politely with approval rather than the kind of mesmerizing charmer who could make people *want* to hear more. He was viewed as a "safe pair of hands" who was best at presenting fairly factual updates and forecasts – at talking through PowerPoint bullet points – to existing clients rather than an inspiring leader who could rouse and win over prospective clients.

I began by working with Anthony on varying the volume, pace and intonation of his speech so that he could portray a broader range of moods and emotions. We also decided that he came across as more energetic when he walked around and used his arms and whole body to act out what he was saying to a greater degree.

Arguably the biggest transformation, though, came from weaving personal stories into his presentations. He began by relating case studies of clients he'd worked with or witnessed. When he became more practised, he even started drawing from his personal life. He spoke about his own career regrets to illustrate how clients should pounce on fleeting opportunities before they disappeared. And to make a point about the importance of planning but being flexible too, he told of the birth of his first child and the joy but also chaos that a baby girl introduced into his life.

Like many people, he had found it difficult to get excited when reciting mere facts and figures. But in talking about his own experiences and what they meant to him, he was able to access a much deeper well of emotions. He showed that he could be funny, sad, courageous, passionate or dramatic – all of which made him so much more engaging and darned entertaining to listen to.

We are all creatures of emotion so much more than logic. While we may understand a rational argument in our heads, we typically respond so much better with our hearts. Who doesn't have hopes, fears, ambitions and desires?

So whether you're pitching a concept, product, vision, noble cause or even yourself to an audience, consider telling more stories. Tell customers about how a product – a car, home, piece of software, whatever – helped a particular customer to live a better life. Tell the story of how your charity helped a single child, an abandoned puppy or a struggling village. Tell interviewers exactly how you made your last organization a better, more successful place.

Tell a good story and people *want* to know what happened. Tell stories and you may find that people can't help but respond.

Onwards and upwards

- Consider that humanity has probably been telling stories for tens of thousands of years. And while few people enjoy being told what to do or sold to, they are invariably much more willing to listen to stories.

- Remember that stories somehow manage to be influential and persuasive often *in spite* of people's better judgement. Most audiences realize that they *should* pay attention to facts and statistics, but still can't help but be swayed by stories.

- Use the "SOAR vividly" phrase to assemble basic but effective stories. Think about the Situation or setting of your story. Describe the Obstacles and the Actions that happened. Finish your story with a Resolution. And don't forget to add in vivid details to help your audience visualize what transpired.

- If you're trying to encourage your audience to change their attitudes or behave in a different way, aim to tell stories involving characters from a similar ingroup (i.e. people with a similar background to your audience). Most people find it easier to empathize with characters like themselves, which leaves them more open to persuasion.

- Keep in mind that an effective story is one in which an audience feels transported away from the real world and into the world of your tale. When you've drafted a story, read it back a couple of times. Is it dynamic and evocative? If not, think about tweaking it – perhaps by adding some more florid language to craft more vivid mental images.

- Finally, remember from our discussion of growth mind-sets (in Chapter 1: Developing a Winning Outlook) that everybody can get better at these skills. You just need to have an open-minded attitude and be ready to work at it.

4
Winning the Job

If at first you do succeed, try something harder.
Ann Landers

This is probably an all-too-familiar story. A couple of years ago, a buddy, whom I'll call Zachary, was feeling intensely frustrated that he wasn't getting the recognition at work he felt he deserved.

But let me backtrack a little. When I first met him at university, Zachary was a looming, burly guy with an unruly shock of muddy-blond hair and a tendency to deliver the most witheringly sarcastic put-downs I'd ever heard. Upon graduating in the mid-1990s, he started his career by taking a job as an accountant with a medium-sized accountancy firm. He specialized in the provision of tax advice and over the next decade was promoted a handful of times.

He occasionally felt discouraged by the fact that a few of his colleagues were promoted more rapidly. But he was otherwise happy with his life: he got married, bought a house with his wife and now has two energetic, wide-eyed daughters. And at least he was still making headway in his career, so he stuck with the job.

He was promoted to become a senior manager about six years ago. But then his career stalled. Many of his fellow senior managers were offered a further promotion to become partners with the firm. But not Zachary. The first year, the executive board in charge of electing new partners told him that they didn't think he was quite ready.

He was told that he needed to build stronger relationships with clients. So he worked on his client relationships. Only to be informed the next year that he hadn't done enough.

He worked harder over the following 12 months, putting in longer and longer hours. But guess what? Again, the executive board told him that he hadn't quite done enough.

Zachary eventually decided to look for a new job. He got in touch with recruiters and alerted contacts within his network that he was actively seeking a move. Within eight months he landed himself a bigger job as an associate partner in a competing firm. He got a whopping 26 per cent pay rise. And a year later, when he was promoted to become a full partner, his pay package more than *doubled*.

So let's think about your situation for a moment. Would *you* like a pay rise?

Silly question probably. You probably feel you are ready for a promotion. You may know that you have the skills and talents that would allow you to take on more responsibility – to manage a bigger budget, team or project. But perhaps you feel hacked off that your current boss is unable to recognize your value and give you what you want.

If so, it's time to wake up. The unfortunate reality is that the quickest way to get a pay rise and more responsibility is invariably to get a new job. Bosses often get stuck in the past: they may have got used to having you around. Maybe they still see you as the office junior. Bosses are risk-averse when it comes to promoting employees they already have. It's usually much easier to get a pay rise by taking a bigger role elsewhere than by waiting, waiting, hoping for your bosses to notice that you're better than the person you used to be.

Maybe you're already on the hunt for a job elsewhere or just thinking about one in the months or even years to come. Whatever the case, in this chapter I'll take you through what science – as well as my own deep experience of working with both employers and candidates – can share about finding a lovely new job.

Rather than telling you stuff that you already know, though, I'll share with you some peculiar but useful findings about the interview tactics that get people hired. We'll debunk myths about body language during job interviews. We'll uncover the real power of informal networks when it comes to landing a job. And, once you've been offered that new job, we'll discuss a sneaky but proven tactic for negotiating a bigger salary.

The quickest way to get a pay rise and more responsibility is invariably to get a new job.

Impressing at interview

Ever heard the saying that it's not *what* you say, it's *how* you say it that counts? In support of this idea, there's a widespread claim in many pop psychology books stating that:

- 55 per cent of what we communicate is done through body language – our posture, movements and facial expressions

- 38 per cent is through tone of voice

- and a mere 7 per cent through words.

This 55–38–7 rule is based on a classic piece of research which many life coaches and trainers have misinterpreted.[1] If we were to believe the claim, it suggests that 93 per cent of the impact we have on others is nothing to do with the words we choose. But if you stop to think about the claim, it can only be utter rubbish.

Imagine that two candidates, Peter and Patricia, are interviewed for the same job. Patricia talks about her relevant skills and experience but does so in a quiet, somewhat uncertain tone. She makes little eye contact and clears her throat a few too many times. She sits in a slightly hunched fashion and, by the way she keeps shifting in her seat and running her hands down the sides of her skirt, comes across as a little nervous.

On the other hand, Peter speaks with a loud, assertive voice. He makes unflinching eye contact and sits with a confident, upright posture in his chair. He makes expansive gestures with his hands when he talks. He smiles frequently, flaunting a mouthful of movie star white teeth. Unfortunately, in answer to every interview question, he replies: "I'm a fraud and a liar as I have no relevant skills or experience for this job."

The misquoted 55–38–7 rule would suggest that Peter would get the job based on his strong body language and tone of voice. But obviously his words would have quite a powerful impact on us – certainly more than the meagre 7 per cent they are supposed to have on the interviewer.

But we don't have to rely only on intellectual games to debunk the 55–38–7 rule. A study by University of Southern Mississippi psychologist James Hollandsworth and colleagues used a statistical technique, known as discriminant analysis, to examine the relative importance of seven different factors on interview performance. The researchers looked at:

- Eye contact.
- Body posture.
- Loudness of voice.
- Fluency of speech.
- Appropriateness of content.
- Personal appearance.
- Composure.

Looking at that list, which do *you* think would matter most and least?

Hollandsworth's results showed that the single-most-prominent factor was the appropriateness of content (i.e. the answers that candidates gave), the stories and explanations they used to elaborate on their skills and experience. The next two most important factors were fluency of speech (i.e. speaking without too much hesitation) and composure (i.e. coming across as calm and confident). All of the other variables were of much less importance.[2]

Hopefully, none of that should shock you much. But the larger point is this: your answers matter the most. Body language matters far less than you may think. So putting time into preparing your interview answers would be your best investment rather than obsessing unduly about how you come across.

Body language matters far less than you may think.

Answering tough interview questions

If you think back to the job interviews you've attended, what's the strangest, most unnerving question you've ever been asked?

I've heard interviewers ask all manner of questions, including: "If you could have dinner with any six people living or dead, who would they be and why?" and "What's the most crushing experience you've ever faced in your life?"

Thankfully, such odd questions are actually pretty rare. The vast majority of interviewers stick to the same kinds of questions time and time again. In fact, researchers have argued that most employers are actually looking for just eight broad skills – sometimes called the "great eight" competencies.[3]

Of course, some roles may require special technical skills, but most of these "great eight" skills are simply human abilities that should be as relevant to office workers and managers as to shop assistants, teachers, scientists or even workers on an oilrig. So if you can prepare stories to tell about these eight skills, or competencies, you could feel pretty confident about making a good impression.

Briefly, the eight broad skills are:

- **Deciding and leading:** taking control of situations and exercising leadership. The "deciding" bit involves taking responsibility (rather than waiting for others to decide what to do), calculating the risks associated with different courses of action, making decisions and initiating action. The "leading" bit means giving direction and guidance to others and then coaching and supervising them to get things done.

- **Supporting and cooperating:** helping others and showing respect for people, whether they are colleagues or customers. This means becoming a good team player by listening to others, trying to understand how different folks may be motivated by particular things and adapting to the team. Cooperation entails communicating relevant information to others and consulting them, as well as behaving ethically and showing empathy, tolerance and consideration.

- **Interacting and presenting:** communicating in a confident and credible manner, whether on a one-to-one basis, in groups or when giving presentations. This also includes being able to build rapport, persuade, influence and negotiate effectively with people.

- **Analyzing and interpreting:** evaluating both qualitative and quantitative data to get to the crux of complex problems and issues. This means being able to test assumptions, make appropriate judgements and come up with solutions.

- **Learning and conceptualizing**: researching and gathering information, learning knowledge and then applying it. The "conceptualizing" part includes being able to come up with ideas or innovative products (or services or new ways of working) and successfully introducing change.

- **Organizing and executing**: setting objectives, planning and then managing time and resources in order to accomplish those objectives. This also requires being able to monitor progress, prioritize and take corrective action if things aren't going to plan.

- **Adapting and coping**: being flexible and accommodating when things change. This also means being able to cope with pressure, handle criticism and bounce back after setbacks.

- **Enterprising and performing**: being able to work with energy and enthusiasm until the work is completed. Enterprising individuals have ambition and look for ways to improve themselves too. Enterprising people also have an awareness of business, commerce and the need to control costs.

As you can see, the "great eight" is a slight misnomer. Some of the competencies – for example "deciding and leading" – actually include a couple of sub-skills. But the broader idea is that most organizations want to hire people who have at least a basic level of proficiency across all of these competencies. So it's a good idea to have stories at the ready to illustrate that you have each of these skills.

Telling stories that sell your skills

Hopefully you'll be thinking that we already covered story construction in Chapter 3: Winning the Pitch. And the good news is that we can apply the "SOAR vividly" technique we encountered in that chapter to the "great eight" competencies too.

I recommend flicking back to that earlier chapter for a reminder of the components of the "SOAR vividly" technique. But briefly, you may recall that the idea is to tell stories that cover the situation you encountered, the obstacles you faced, the actions you took and the resolution that occurred. The "vividly" bit means having at least one or two visual, memorable details to bring the story to life.

In order to prepare effective stories for each of the "great eight" competencies, you could try answering the following questions:

"Great eight" competency	Questions for which you may want to have stories ready
Deciding and leading	"Tell us about a time you had to make a difficult decision." "Give me an example of a situation in which you demonstrated leadership over others."
Supporting and cooperating	"Tell us about a time you made a significant contribution to a team." "Talk us through a situation in which you helped a colleague or customer." "Think about an occasion your ethics or values were challenged at work. How did you respond to the situation?"
Interacting and presenting	"Please tell us about an occasion you changed someone's mind." "Tell us about a presentation you gave. How did you prepare and what reaction did you get?"

(Continued)

"Great eight" competency	Questions for which you may want to have stories ready
Analyzing and interpreting	"Can you think of a time you faced a complex problem? Talk us through how you analyzed and dealt with the problem."
Learning and conceptualizing	"Please tell us about a skill or technical topic you had to learn about. How did you learn about it and then apply it?" "Give us an example of something that you created, introduced or changed at work."
Organizing and executing	"Tell us about a project that you managed. Talk us through how you decided what needed to be done and how you made everything happen."
Adapting and coping	"Give us an example of a project you were involved with that changed direction. What did you do in response to the change?" "Tell us about a time you experienced a setback or failure. How did you respond?"
Enterprising and performing	"Tell us about a particularly challenging or tough project that you worked on. How did it make you feel and how did you deal with it?"

So what "SOAR vividly" stories would you use to illustrate each of the "great eight" skills? Clearly, your examples should showcase your abilities in the best possible light, so you may want to spend a little time thinking about situations in which you took the initiative and achieved a successful result. Take a glance back at the short bullet-point descriptions of each competency in the section just above this one to guide your thinking.

Once you have stories for these eight skills, you can use them as the core of your interview approach. Say an interviewer asks you

"What are your strengths?" or opens with "Tell me about yourself", you could list a couple of the skills you believe you have and go on to give an example, "I know I'm very good at planning and organizing projects, for example there was this one time when I . . ."

Go into an interview with good stories to tell and you can feel confident that you'll acquit yourself well.

Or if an interviewer asked you why you thought you would be suited to the job, you could answer by talking about how your talents perfectly matched the requirements of the job: "Your advertisement said that you're looking for someone with exceptional analytical and decision-making skills. That's definitely me because I once . . ." – and then go on to give your "SOAR vividly" story as an example.

I've introduced this technique to dozens and dozens of job hunters, from graduates to senior managers, with terrific results. For instance, I recently coached a warm but soft-spoken 22-year-old graduate called Ameena who was preparing for a decisive interview. She had applied to the top veterinary school in the country the year before but had been turned down. Having waited 12 months for a second chance, she desperately wanted to get it right this time.

When I met her and took her through a mock interview, I quickly grasped that she wasn't articulating her experience well. She had been working as a veterinary volunteer for several months, so on paper had tremendous experience of working with not only animals but also their owners and veterinary staff. But in speaking about her achievements, she spent far too long explaining the situations, the backgrounds to what she had done. And then she pretty much jumped to the resolution, the conclusion of each story. She wasn't giving me a proper indication of what *her* role had been.

I introduced Ameena to the "SOAR vividly" principle and we worked through a couple of her stories together. She had the experience so it was just a case of drawing it out of her and helping her to order her thoughts. I kept asking her, "What was the first difficulty you encountered?" and "Exactly what did you do next?" and then, "What was the next difficulty you encountered?" and so on.

It only took her a single 90-minute coaching session to get the hang of the method. We worked on less than a half-dozen stories together, figuring out the best ways to present her experiences. She went away to write up her other stories herself.

A few months later, I got an email from Ameena. She passed the interview and got on the course. She was en route to her dream career.

Having even top-notch skills and the right experience isn't the same as being able to *articulate* your skills and experience. Figuring out how best to tell your stories may take you a handful of hours. But go into an interview with good stories to tell and you can feel confident that you'll acquit yourself well.

Beguiling interviewers with words

When psychologists first began researching job interviews as far back as the 1940s, they were mostly interested in exploring how interviewers could ask more penetrating questions in order to separate genuinely superior candidates from weaker ones. For example, these studies suggest that structured interviews (in which interviewers formulate their questions beforehand and ask the same questions of different candidates) are generally more useful for spotting good candidates than unstructured interviews (in which interviewers chat to candidates and rely more on their intuition). How employers can interview more effectively isn't the focus of this chapter, but I have written a book on the topic if you're interested – *Successful Interviewing and Recruitment* (Kogan Page).[4]

In the last decade or so, psychologists have shown greater interest in tactics deployed by candidates that help them to get hired. In order to explain how some of these tactics work, I'd encourage you to complete the four short quizzes below. As with any psychological questionnaires, work through the statements in each quiz fairly quickly and answer as honestly as you can.

Quiz A

For each of the four quizzes, think back to the last set of job interviews you had. Please rate the extent to which you agree or disagree with each of the following five statements. Please use a five-point scale where 1 = "strongly disagree" and 5 = "strongly agree".

	1: strongly disagree	2: slightly disagree	3: neither agree nor disagree	4: slightly agree	5: strongly agree
1. I played up the value of positive events that I took credit for.					
2. I described my skills and abilities in an attractive way.					
3. I took charge during the interview to get my main points across.					

(Continued)

	1: strongly disagree	2: slightly disagree	3: neither agree nor disagree	4: slightly agree	5: strongly agree
4. I took credit for positive events even if I was not solely responsible.					
5. I made positive events I was responsible for appear better than they actually were.					

This first quiz measures a candidate interview tactic known as "self-promotion", which involves emphasizing your skills and achievements and perhaps avoiding or downplaying the negative aspects of your career history. It means picking examples and stories to talk about that showcase your successes rather than ones that expose your faults. After all, why tell interviewers anything that's wrong with your application unless they specifically ask?

Surveys have found that *the majority* of job hunters admit to using self-promotion to buoy their chances at interview.[5] And, more importantly, many groups of researchers – including a team led by the influential academic Brian Swider at Mays Business School in Texas – have found that candidates who engage in self-promotion are usually rated more highly by interviewers than those who don't.[6] By carefully choosing the experiences they talk about, self-promoting candidates are typically judged to be the strongest candidates.

How did you rate yourself on self-promotion in the quiz? The more you agreed with the questions in Quiz A, the more you self-promote. And the more you self-promote, the more likely you will be to make a good impression and get offered the job.

If you're wondering how to self-promote more effectively, take a look back at the five statements in Quiz A. Self-promotion is about taking control of what you wish to talk about rather than being subjected to the whims of the interviewer. It's about being assertive about what you've achieved rather than hoping that an interviewer may ask you the right question.

How can you do that? Prepare "SOAR vividly" stories, of course. And then find every opportunity to swerve onto those stories during the course of an interview to highlight your best side.

> The more you self-promote, the more likely you will be to make a good impression and get offered the job.

Quiz B

As with the last quiz, rate your agreement or disagreement with each statement in relation to the last employment interviews you attended. Please use a five-point scale where 1 = "strongly disagree" and 5 = "strongly agree".

	1: strongly disagree	2: slightly disagree	3: neither agree nor disagree	4: slightly agree	5: strongly agree
1. I exaggerated the impact of my performance in my past jobs.					

(Continued)

	1: strongly disagree	2: slightly disagree	3: neither agree nor disagree	4: slightly agree	5: strongly agree
2. I exaggerated my future goals.					
3. During the interview, I distorted my answers to emphasize what the interviewer was looking for.					
4. I distorted my work experience to fit the interviewer's view of the position.					
5. I enhanced my fit with the job in terms of my attitudes, values or beliefs.					
6. During the interview, I distorted my answers based on the comments or reactions of the interviewer.					

Quizzes B and C measure similar candidate tactics, so have a look at Quiz C and then I'll explain about both afterwards.

Quiz C

Again, rate your agreement or disagreement with each statement in relation to the last employment interviews you attended. Please use a five-point scale where 1 = "strongly disagree" and 5 = "strongly agree".

	1: strongly disagree	2: slightly disagree	3: neither agree nor disagree	4: slightly agree	5: strongly agree
1. I fabricated examples to show my fit with the organization.					
2. I told stories that contained both real and fictional work experiences.					
3. I stretched the truth to give a good answer.					
4. I invented some work situations or accomplishments that did not really occur.					
5. I used other people's experiences to create answers when I did not have good experiences of my own.					
6. I described team accomplishments as primarily my own.					

Quiz B measures an interview tactic known as "slight image creation", which is a more aggressive tactic than self-promotion. Look back at Quiz B and you'll see verbs such as "exaggerated", "distorted" and "enhanced". Slight image creation therefore involves overstating, embellishing or adapting answers beyond a reasonable description of the truth in order to fit the job. So candidates may deviate slightly but purposely from the truth to either emphasize desirable characteristics or foster a better impression.

Quiz C measures a stronger version of the tactic known as "extensive image creation". Look back at the wording of the statements in Quiz C and you'll see more aggressive verbs such as "fabricated", "invented" and "used other people's experiences to create answers". Extensive image creation involves intentionally constructing stories about non-existent experiences, inventing accomplishments that never occurred and stealing other people's stories. If slight image creation is a mild form of deception or dishonesty, then extensive image creation could be viewed as blatant lying or deceit.

The more you agreed with the statements in either Quiz B or Quiz C, the more you are likely to have engaged in either slight image creation or extensive image creation, respectively.[7] But is that good or bad when it comes to trying to get a job?

The same study by Brian Swider and his colleagues at Texas A&M University found that both slight image creation *and* extensive image creation led to *worse* interview scores. In other words, misrepresent your experience or suitability for the job and you may *reduce* your chances of getting hired.

Swider and his team suggest that self-promotion (as covered in Quiz A) leads to better interview ratings because it merely involves highlighting actual skills and experiences. It's about talking about what you genuinely did, but doing so by framing it in the best way.

On the other hand, both of the image creation tactics may backfire because they are forms of lying. As such, interviewees have to work much harder to control not only what they are saying but also their emotions and other behaviours, such as facial tics, tone of voice and so on in an attempt to make their lies seem believable.

It's possible that candidates who engage in either form of image creation may struggle to keep their emotions or behaviours in check and therefore come across as less personable and less confident because they have to work harder cognitively to keep their stories straight. Or maybe they get rated poorly because they are simply more likely to get caught out.

The clear moral then: even though it may occasionally be tempting to exaggerate or lie, we may end up harming our own chances rather than enhancing them.

Misrepresent your experience or suitability for the job and you may reduce your chances of getting hired.

Quiz D

	1: strongly disagree	2: slightly disagree	3: neither agree nor disagree	4: slightly agree	5: strongly agree
1. I praised the organization.					
2. I complimented the interviewer or organization.					

(Continued)

	1: strongly disagree	2: slightly disagree	3: neither agree nor disagree	4: slightly agree	5: strongly agree
3. I discussed non-job-related topics about which the interviewer and I shared similar opinions.					
4. I discussed interests I shared in common with the interviewer.					
5. I indicated my interest for the position and the company.					
6. I found out what kind of person the organization was seeking and I explained how I would fit in.					
7. I indicated my enthusiasm for working for this organization.					
8. I smiled a lot or used other friendly non-verbal behaviours.					

The eight statements that make up Quiz D measure a tactic known as "ingratiation", which involves flattering the organization and expressing beliefs or attitudes held by the interviewer or the organization. For example, if an interviewer mentions in passing a personal dislike for the game of football, a savvy candidate who decides to engage in ingratiation could say, "Oh yes, I can't stand it either." Or a candidate may say something positive about the organization such as, "Well, you're definitely the top law firm in the country" or "I've applied to six other firms, but yours is the one I aspire to work for most because . . ."

So if you agreed with the statements in Quiz D, you are likely to engage in more ingratiation than people who disagreed with the statements. But is that good or bad? What do you think?

When I first came across ingratiation as a candidate tactic for manipulating interviewers, I thought that surely interviewers would be able to see through such transparent attempts on the part of candidates to flatter and sweet-talk them. But I was wrong.

Researchers such as Chad Higgins at the University of Washington and Timothy Judge at the University of Florida have found that ingratiation actually has not only a positive effect but also a powerful one. Candidates who engaged in ingratiation were judged to be significantly stronger candidates and therefore were more likely to get offered the job than those who didn't.[8] Making an effort to appear interested and upbeat pays off.

Making an effort to appear interested and upbeat pays off.

Now you may be wondering: isn't ingratiation just another, perhaps milder, form of deception? For example, some would say that it's wrong to pretend that you like or dislike something simply because an interviewer expresses an opinion.

But isn't at least some of success at work about pretending? In dealing with customers, clients and even bosses, many people report portraying a role rather than being entirely themselves.

Employees ranging from shop assistants and restaurant waiting staff to airline cabin crew and hairdressers frequently have to hide their true emotions and project a more upbeat image than they may actually be feeling. Financial advisers, lawyers, doctors, psychotherapists and teachers may at times feel frustrated or bored with their clients, patients or students and need to put on a professional demeanour.

Many of us have at least occasionally wanted to scream at our bosses and tell them how unreasonable they're being. However, we know that it's generally a better idea to keep our true thoughts and feelings to ourselves.

In fact, business school professors have even found evidence suggesting that people who adopt self-serving interview tactics such as self-promotion or ingratiation don't just get more job offers; *they may actually be more successful on the job too*.[9] These academics suggest that being able to follow an interviewer's lead and showcase your best side during an interview means being able to put on a show with customers, clients and colleagues too.

Taking all of this research together, we know with some certainty that both self-promotion (Quiz A) and ingratiation (Quiz D) pay off. Of course, I'm not saying that you *should* or *must* engage in such tactics. All I'm doing is reporting on what research tells us. Whether you feel comfortable engaging in such manoeuvres is ultimately and entirely up to you.

> ## Tweaking your interview persona
>
> You could think of self-promotion as putting forward the best aspects of yourself and ingratiation as being positive and complimentary. If you're looking to get hired more quickly, how could you change your behaviour in your next interview?
>
> Take a look back at the individual statements in both Quiz A and Quiz D to see exactly what each tactic consists of. What specific behaviours could you adopt in your next interview?

Using body language to best effect

Earlier on I recounted a study by James Hollandsworth and colleagues which found that our words and fluency are the two biggest factors in determining interview success. But that doesn't mean that body language doesn't matter at all.

To reiterate, the most important step in preparing for an interview is to ensure that you've got killer "SOAR vividly" stories to tell. That looks after what you could say. Next comes practising them by rehearsing them out loud enough times so that you tell your stories in a composed and fluent fashion. Only then should you think about your body language.

I'll cover body language only briefly, because you'll probably be surprised by none of the findings in the research:

- Candidates who offer firm handshakes tend to get better interview ratings than those who don't. This is equally true for men and women candidates. Candidates who offer weak hand-shakes tend to be viewed as more shy and neurotic.[10]

■ In a different study, candidates received higher interview ratings when they exhibited certain non-verbal behaviours such as more eye contact, smiling, hand gestures and head nodding – but *only* when the verbal content of their answers was good. When candidates' interview responses were judged to be poor, it didn't matter how much eye contact, smiling and so on they displayed.[11] So eye contact, smiling and other body language cues do make a difference – but yet again this study shows that *what* you say still matters most.

■ Contrary to popular opinion, it does *not* matter whether you sit with your arms folded in front of you or even behind you and hooked over the back of the chair. Even though we're often told that sitting with crossed arms may be a sign of defensiveness, it seems that interviewers don't notice. British researchers Ray Forbes and Paul Jackson also found that interviewers don't notice candidates' legs either – whether you sit with your legs in a crossed or uncrossed position or whether you sit still or move your legs about.[12]

■ The same study by Forbes and Jackson also found that body posture doesn't influence interviewers' ratings either. Whether candidates sat back, sat forward or sat upright made no difference.

When I'm coaching job hunters on how to sell themselves effectively during interviews, they sometimes say that they are worried about having to choose the right words *and* control their body language at the same time. But the good news is that you may not have to for very long.

Several studies show that interviewers tend to be unduly swayed by their first impressions. In one investigation, for example, an elite squad of researchers led by business school professor Murray Barrick asked interviewers to chat informally to candidates for three minutes before interviewing them more formally for between 30 to 45 minutes using a set of agreed questions. The academics found that interviewers' first impressions at the three-minute mark were strongly related to the scores that they gave candidates after the full interview. In other words, those swashbuckling candidates who made a strong impact during those first few minutes generally received higher interview rating scores; candidates who fumbled those crucial first three minutes tended to receive much lower interview ratings.[13]

The lesson: work extra hard during those first few minutes. Offer a firm handshake. Make strong eye contact. Flash your teeth in a big smile and find something positive to say about the organization. Work at being particularly eloquent and effusive for a mere three minutes and you set yourself up for the rest of your interview.

Studies show that interviewers tend to be unduly influenced by their first impressions.

Getting invited to more interviews

What can you do if it's not the interview stage that's frustrating you but the fact that you wished you could get invited to more interviews?

You've probably heard the adage that it's not *what* you know but *who* you know. But is it true? Does science support what we're all being told about the power of networking and informal word of mouth as a way of getting hired?

Before we ponder the evidence, let me ask you a question about *your* present employment: by what means were *you* first informed about your current job?

Here are the six options you can choose from:

- By applying to the employer directly.
- By inserting or answering adverts in newspapers, TV, radio, or online.
- Through employment or vocational guidance agencies.
- Through family, friends or other contacts.
- Started own business or joined family business.
- Other.

More or less that same question has been asked of tens of thousands of people in more than a dozen European countries in a major survey called the European Community Household Panel. Analyzing the data, Michele Pellizzari, a world-leading professor of economics at Bocconi University in Italy, published a paper in 2010 finding that 22 per cent of people in the UK said that they found jobs through personal contacts. So that's more than one in five Brits finding work through family, friends or other contacts.

In many other European countries, the proportion was even higher: 24 per cent of individuals in Ireland, Belgium and Austria said that they got hired through informal contacts – nearly one in four people. And a staggering 32 per cent of the French – nearly one in three – said that they got hired through unofficial rather than formal job channels.[14]

You can read into the data whatever you like about employers' attitudes about mentoring, sponsorship and outright nepotism across Europe. But you can't escape the fact that networking really is a phenomenally important part of our job seeking toolkit.

When I mention the importance of exploiting personal contacts to job seekers, they sometimes say, "I don't know anyone important!" But Pellizzari's study suggests that personal contacts benefit just about everyone. His analysis found that relative youngsters at the start of their careers in their late teens or early 20s were equally likely to gain advantage from personal contacts as seasoned workers in their 50s and 60s. And informal networking was as indispensable for low-earning manual workers as high-flying managers and professionals.

So there's no excuse not to network. A school leaver looking for a first job on an assembly line is as likely to find work through personal contacts as a chief executive casting around for one last job before retirement. In fact, refusing to network – to ask friends and family for help and recommendations in finding that next job – would be like running a race but deciding not to use your left leg.

Study after study tells us that personal contacts, informal networks and recommendations matter. We know categorically that job seekers who network tend to receive more job offers than job seekers who respond solely to advertisements they found online, in the press or via recruitment agencies.[15]

It makes sense that networking should work when you think about it. Companies can get hundreds of applications for every vacancy. And the best way for you as a candidate to get an edge over the competition is to have friends who can point you to job openings, recommend you for interview and advise you on your best route forward. If you're looking for your next job, can you afford *not* to network?

Refusing to network would be like running a race but deciding not to use your left leg.

Thinking about "reaching out" rather than "networking"

I hope that I've debunked some of the mystique around networking. Your network is nothing more than your collection of friends, colleagues and acquaintances. And networking is nothing more than getting in touch with people you know to ask for advice and recommendations.

In fact, I don't like the verb "to network" – it sounds like something cold and mechanical. Rather than speaking about "networking", I prefer to call it "reaching out".

Because all you need to do is reach out to the people you already know – and ask them for a few minutes of their time. If you don't like the idea of networking, drop the word from your vocabulary and think in terms of reaching out instead.

Think of it this way. Your friends – your mates, pals, buddies – like you, love you and *want* to help you out. If you had to approach just three friends for advice and support in your job hunt, who would they be?

Getting help from a network

Many folks don't like the idea of networking. But when they try it, they often find that it's both incredibly worthwhile and easier than they first suspected.

I just finished working with a job hunter I'll call Veronica. An experienced but timid accountant in her mid-40s with wavy chestnut-brown hair, she lost her job as part of a company-wide restructuring about a year before we met. She had some savings and so took a few months off to travel the world, going scuba diving off the coast of Thailand and then meandering around galleries and museums in Italy. When she eventually got home, she started looking for work. But after more than six months and zero interviews, she came to me for help.

One of the problems she faced was that she was trying to move from the publishing industry into the technology sector. She felt that publishing was a declining industry and she wanted to give herself more options by moving into the world of online commerce. Unfortunately, she had no experience of working for a tech firm.

Veronica had been relatively passive in her job search so far. She had contacted a couple of recruitment consultants and waited (in vain) for them to put her forward for jobs. And she had responded to dozens of online advertisements without success. But she had done almost no active networking or reaching out to the people she knew.

When I suggested that she would almost certainly benefit from using her network more, she was reluctant. Like many people, she felt that she didn't have a network. Plus, she imagined that networking would involve attending conferences and cocktail parties and having to schmooze and strike up conversations with endless strangers.

But I explained that a network is nothing more than a group of friends who occasionally help each other out professionally. And then I asked her: "Do you have any friends?"

Of course, she replied that she did.

So I told Veronica that we were going to think about how her existing friends could help her out. I began by turning to a new page in my notebook and drawing up a table.

Name	Relationship	Usefulness	Action

I then invited Veronica to bring to mind the names of five people she knew – not just colleagues who may be useful but friends, family, the first names that popped into her head. We wrote these names into the left-hand "Name" column of the table.

To fill the "Relationship" and "Usefulness" columns, I then asked her to rate each person based on how well she knew them and how useful each person could be. I proposed using between one and three stars in the "Relationship" column and between one to three ticks for "Usefulness".

So three stars in the "Relationship" column meant that she knew someone extremely well – she was great friends with that person. Two stars meant she knew that individual fairly well. And one star meant she knew him or her only passingly.

Likewise, a name received three ticks if that person was fairly senior and worked in the right industry. In contrast, one tick meant that the person was perhaps either more junior or didn't work in the right industry.

And so our table looked as follows:

Name	Relationship	Usefulness	Action
Mark Brewer	***	✓✓	
Timothy Chang	**	✓✓	
Evan Spence	***	✓	
Nasreen Khan	**	✓✓✓	
Jake Cavendish	*	✓✓✓	

Next, I asked Veronica to tell me a little about each person and then to think about what specific help each individual could be able to give her. What introductions would they be able to make on her behalf? What advice or practical support could each person offer?

Talking through the names she had written down, she explained that Mark was one of her best friends from her university days. She had known him for more than 20 years. He was also an accountant, so Veronica decided that he could help her by critiquing her CV and helping her to rewrite it in as appealing a fashion as possible.

Timothy was a close confidant and an accountant at the publishing company she had left. She felt that he would be more than willing to run through a mock interview with her, perhaps over a couple of glasses of wine one evening.

Evan was another university friend of long standing that Veronica cherished and trusted deeply. However, Evan received only one tick in the "Usefulness" column because he wasn't an accountant and he didn't work in the technology sector either. But as he was such a close friend, Veronica decided that she could simply tell him about her situation and ask for referrals to anyone who could be useful, for example friends or colleagues of Evan's who worked in finance or technology.

Nasreen was a friend of Veronica's from an earlier job when they had both worked at a magazine company. Nasreen worked in sales but had successfully made the leap into a senior sales role working at a software company (i.e. in the tech industry). So Veronica decided that she could talk to Nasreen in order to learn about the tech world in general. Veronica felt that Nasreen could potentially be willing to introduce her to the accountants within Nasreen's current tech employer too.

And Jake was Veronica's ex-boss. She had left the company on good terms with him. She said that he wasn't exactly a close friend but could be instrumental in giving her advice and potentially referring her to senior accountants within other organizations.

So finally, we populated the table to look as follows:

Name	Relationship	Usefulness	Action
Mark Brewer	***	✓✓	Help with CV
Timothy Chang	**	✓✓	Practice interview
Evan Spence	***	✓	Referrals to other people?
Nasreen Khan	**	✓✓✓	Ask about tech industry
Jake Cavendish	*	✓✓✓	Advice, recommendations

Doing that took perhaps 10 to 15 minutes. But I suggested to Veronica that she might want to work on her own to write down the names of 50 people in total and then to go through the same exercise, ranking each person in terms of her relationship with them, their usefulness to her, and so on.

Veronica wasn't entirely convinced about reaching out to her network for help, but I gave her a final piece of advice to help her build her confidence and skill in networking. I told her to begin by getting in touch with the people with whom she had the strongest relationships but who were the weakest in terms of usefulness. That way, she could ease herself into the task fairly gently – she only needed to pick up the phone or meet up with her closest friends, the people she already felt most comfortable with.

So Evan (three stars but one tick) should be Veronica's first contact, followed by Mark. Next would be Timothy, then Nasreen. Only when she had practised her networking patter and built up her confidence would she need to get in touch with more challenging contacts, such as Jake.

Tapping your own network

So if you need to reach out to your network for help in landing your next job, start by drawing up the same kind of table:

Name	Relationship	Usefulness	Action

Next, write down the names of *at least* 50 people. Go through your address book or emails. Don't leave names off your list because you think someone won't be useful or because you don't think they will help. Just get names down.

Then, as Veronica did, think about the strength of your relationship with them. Close friends, who support and love you, get three stars; acquaintances get one.

Consider how useful each person could be too. Someone who is senior, knowledgeable or well connected may warrant three ticks. Someone less helpful may be two ticks or even just one.

Finally, go back through your list thinking about what specific request you could make of each individual. And then you're ready to start reaching out, to pick up the telephone or ping off emails with the aim of meeting up in person.

This isn't by any means a definitive list, but here are some of the commonest ways that my clients have sometimes decided to tap their networks for help:

- Practice with mock interviews – either by allowing friends to ask you whatever questions they like or by suggesting questions to your friends that you'd like to practise answering.

- Help with your written applications. If you're not getting invited to as many interviews as you would like, it may be worth asking sensible friends (especially those who either work in human resources or may have interviewed in the past) for advice on your CV or résumé and covering letters.

- Information about a role, company or industry. Say you're wanting to switch careers to become a teacher. A sensible first step would be to ask friends who were teachers for insight and advice. Or say you would like to work for a particular company or within a different industry, again you might wish to ask friends who worked there for guidance.

- Introductions to other people. Suppose you aspired to work with a company called Atticus Engineering and needed to find out more about the company and a possible route in. Even if you didn't know anyone who worked at Atticus, you could ask friends if they knew anyone who worked at the firm or even within the same industry.

OK. That's listing and categorizing your network done. Time now to actually pick up the phone, ping off a few emails and start meeting people.

Reaching out for real

So far we've covered listing and categorizing your network. Now what?

Yes, it's time to actually pick up the phone, fire off a few emails and start meeting people.

Many of my clients agree that it's a good idea to begin by approaching your closest buddies (those three-star contacts) first. Your best mates won't mind if you haven't formulated your career objectives clearly. They will forgive you if you don't come across as perfectly confident or competent.

Only then can you reach out to two-star people and finally your more distant one-star acquaintances. That way, you get to build your confidence and finesse at reaching out one meeting at a time. You discover how to phrase your requests better. You learn how to ask for introductions or recommendations without coming across as too needy. You get better and better while practising on closer friends so that you're a finely honed networker when it becomes time to approach the one-star acquaintances who may have less time for you.

So who will you start with? Look back at your list and pick out three people. Make a pledge to reach out to them within the next 24 hours. That may involve sending out an email or making a quick phone call. But whatever you choose to do, *just get started.*

I'm not saying that you have to work your way through *all* of your three-star contacts before moving on. If you feel after a couple of conversations that you've got your patter worked out and that you're sure you come across as professional and focused, move on to your lower-starred but more useful friends (i.e. those with more ticks). The point here is to practise on low-risk friends until you feel ready to contact more distant acquaintances. That may take only a handful or perhaps a few more attempts at reaching out to different people. Go at your own pace.

Practise on low-risk friends until you feel ready to contact more distant acquaintances.

Finally, remember that between 20 and 40 per cent of people get jobs through informal channels, personal contacts and reaching out to their networks. Give it a go.

Building up your network

OK, so perhaps you're not looking for a new job right now. But that doesn't mean that you may not need to in the near future. More and more people are investing in their networks as a career insurance policy for when they may need to look for that bigger, sexier role.

Networking researchers Monica Forret and Sherry Sullivan suggest that we should all be engaging in 30 separate networking behaviours.[16] Yes, 30!

But who can keep track of so many different activities? Instead, I've gone through their list and selected the 10 simplest, most effective activities.

So if you want to bulk up your network a little, try to:

- Volunteer for committee assignments.

- Send cards, newspaper clippings, emails, etc. to keep in touch with colleagues.

- Attend meetings of professional or trade organizations.

- Assist colleagues who ask for your help.

- Socialize with peers in your profession or trade.

- Volunteer for community groups.

- Offer your special talents or expertise without requiring payment.

- Become involved in promoting a personal cause, e.g. increasing literacy, preventing breast cancer, helping the elderly.

- Attend and participate in community events.

- Meet people who share your interest in a hobby or athletic activity.

Making a commitment to reach out

Nothing on that list of ten networking activities should surprise you. But then the point about networking isn't that it is intellectually challenging. There are no secrets to be revealed that magically allow people to become better networkers.

You've probably suspected all along the kinds of activities you need to do in order to build up your network. It's just a case of putting it into practice.

So here's your opportunity. From that list of ten, pick out at least *three* actions you pledge to take. What actions strike you

(*Continued*)

as being easy or perhaps enjoyable? Aim to find things you'd *like* to do as opposed to choosing things you feel you *must* do.

Once you've got an idea, turn it into a specific commitment. Decide *what* you will do and *when* you will do it. Go on, jot them down here:

-
-
-

I work as a business psychologist but I know that I sometimes get a bit lax about maintaining and extending my network. So my three actions would be to:

- Attend the next annual conference of the Association of Business Psychologists, a two-day event.

- Spend a half-hour every Monday afternoon emailing friends and business acquaintances with some snippet of news, enquiring about projects I know they're working on or making helpful suggestions and recommendations.

- Make it a priority to meet at least two contacts weekly – prospective clients, current clients or past clients – over lunch, coffee, breakfast, whatever, to chat and listen to what they're working on.

What would your three actions be?

Asking for a bigger salary (and receiving it)

To finish off this chapter, let's look ahead to the moment you receive the job offer that you've been chasing. You should rightly feel proud of yourself, but it isn't *quite* time to celebrate yet. You still need to wring out the best possible pay package before signing on the dotted line. And now – when an employer wants you but doesn't yet have you – is the unreservedly best time to ask for more money.

Before I explain about an easy – and, again, scientifically proven – technique for securing a better deal for yourself, imagine for a moment that you are not a candidate looking for a job but an employer seeking to hire someone. Suppose you run a business and have been looking to recruit an administrative assistant. After interviewing a half-dozen candidates, you've decided to offer the job to a professional, friendly and competent woman named Lydia.

You invite Lydia back for a final meeting to discuss how much you will pay her. You already know from your initial interview that she is currently earning £29,000. After exchanging pleasantries, you broach the topic by asking: "So, Lydia, how much will it cost for you to leave your job and come work for us?"

She laughs and replies: "Well, you already know I like your company but I'm only willing to leave if you pay me £100,000 a year!"

She winks and you both chuckle about the preposterous sum. You know it's a joke. You're not going to let her ridiculous number affect your judgement, right?

Wrong. Because research suggests that you will probably end up paying her a salary of around £3,000 more than she would otherwise have got.

Why?

It all comes down to a psychological phenomenon known as "anchoring". Research tells us that people who are presented with a number – *any* number, even if it's a totally irrelevant number – tend to be influenced by that number in their decision-making.

American researcher Todd Thorsteinson presented exactly the same recruitment scenario to university students in a 2011 experiment. Just as I did, he asked his participants to imagine that they were employers looking to hire an administrative assistant.

To begin with, all of the participants were told that the candidate – a woman – had been invited back for a salary negotiation. And they were all told that she was currently earning $29,000.

But here's the intriguing part. Without their knowledge, the participants were randomly allocated into one of three groups.

The first group were then told that the candidate had been asked what salary she wanted and responded by saying: "Would like $100,000, but really I am just looking for something that is fair."

A second group of participants were told that, in response to a question about her salary expectations, she said: "Would work for $1, but really I am just looking for something that is fair."

The third group of participants were given no additional information. Remember, though, that they had been told the candidate's current salary was $29,000.

The researcher then asked the participants in each group to say how much they would offer her to work for them. So what happened?

When the candidate joked that she wanted $100,000, the participants offered her in excess of $35,000. But when she self-deprecatingly said that she would work for a single dollar, the participants punished her by offering her in the region of $31,000.

When participants were given no further information, they offered her around $32,000.[17]

Spelling it out then, the additional sums of money mentioned by the candidate acted as anchors, affecting the participants' decisions without their conscious knowledge. A high anchor of $100,000 – even though it was an implausibly high salary and mentioned only in passing as a joke – anchored participants' decisions at one end of the scale and pushed their offers higher. Similarly, a low anchor of $1 – again, it was rhetoric rather than a serious comment – anchored participants' judgement at the other end of the scale and pulled their offers lower.

Anchoring is one of the strangest and most robust phenomena in psychology, and has been demonstrated in scores of studies.[18] But the point I want to make is that anchoring *works*. Mention a high figure or a low sum early on in any negotiation or sales transaction and people end up changing their behaviour – and quite without realizing it.

So what's the lesson for job hunters from Todd Thorsteinson's study? In a salary discussion, it pays to mention a really high salary figure first. That way, you anchor the employer's expectations to a higher figure. And when you ultimately agree to something more reasonable, you will probably end up with a salary that's a good deal higher than you would otherwise have got.

But make sure that you get in a mention of that super-high figure first. If the employer mentions a disappointingly low figure first, the discussion could get anchored in the other direction and drag your final salary down.

And remember to state your request as a joke! You don't want an employer to think that your implausibly high figure is a deadly serious request and storm out of the discussion.[19]

In a salary discussion, it pays to mention a really high salary figure first.

To sum up then, Thorsteinson's research suggests that you could potentially earn an additional 10 per cent more simply by making a seemingly frivolous, jokey comment about how much you want. Think about that: *10 per cent.* Would that be worth trying?

Onwards and upwards

- Despite myths about the importance of body language, remember that it's actually *what* you say that matters most during job interviews. Work out "SOAR vividly" stories you can tell about the so-called great eight competencies and you will be able to talk assertively and confidently about your skills and experience.

- Research suggests that candidates who engage in the interview tactics of self-promotion and ingratiation tend to get rated more highly by interviewers. Research also tells us that candidates who distort the truth or tell brazen lies get poorer interview ratings – perhaps because interviewers can detect that something's not quite right. So think carefully about how you present yourself during interviews.

- First impressions really do count when it comes to interviews. Think about those all-important first few minutes. Offer a strong handshake, smile and have something positive or complimentary to say about the organization.

- Research by top economists also tells us that networking works. Many jobs are filled by word of mouth, recommendations and other informal channels. But remember that networking is nothing more than reaching out to ask friends and acquaintances for information, advice and referrals. Reach out a little more and you may significantly ratchet up your chances of getting your next job.

- Remember that all of these skills can be developed and honed, no matter how good you are at them right now. Recall the research on the gifts versus growth mind-sets (from Chapter 1: Developing a Winning Outlook) telling us that we can all learn and get better so long as we work hard and persist.

- Finally, make the most of salary discussions by harnessing the anchoring effect. Get in a jokey mention of an implausibly high salary expectation and you may well end up extracting a higher salary from an employer than you would otherwise have got.

5

Winning the Race

The man who starts out simply with the idea of getting rich won't succeed; you must have a larger ambition.
John D. Rockefeller

What would you say were the rules of career success, the rules that allowed certain people to win the career race?

Work hard, you might say. Do your tasks and duties to the best of your ability. Take the initiative and contribute to the team.

Yes, all of those matter. But only to a degree. And mostly when people are in the very earliest years of their careers.

The main problem is that a lot of people don't know the real rules of the game. Or, to be more precise, the rules change midway on the journey – but no one bothers to tell you when or *how* they changed. Doesn't seem terribly fair, does it?

Things were so much easier when we were kids. The rules of scholastic success were pretty straightforward. Every time we had a test, assignment or exam, we simply had to put in the hours. Learn the material thoroughly and you'd do better in a test; work diligently on an assignment and you'd get a better grade. On the other hand, leave the work till the last minute and you'd likely do not so well or fail entirely.

Essentially, the more effort and work we put into our schoolwork, the better the results we got. It wasn't rocket science.

And the same principle held out when we started out in our careers too. Work hard and you do well. Do what you're told, pay attention to detail, spend longer on the work, get more tasks done – that's the route to success in those early years.

Then the instruction manual gets rewritten. And folks who thought they were succeeding suddenly find themselves falling behind, being held back or forced out entirely.

I've met accountants who were upset that they didn't get promoted even after they did all of their paperwork correctly and kept their clients happy. I've coached lawyers, software engineers, scientists and management consultants who all grumbled about their lack of advancement despite being experts in their fields and often more technically talented than the colleagues who were leapfrogging them.

So with this chapter, I intend to remedy the situation for the many people who don't realize that there's a new playbook for sustained success at work. I'm going to take the previously mysterious, unfathomable rules and make everything clear once and for all. If hard work alone can't get you to the top, what can?

We'll begin by looking at the red-hot topic of organizational savvy, a skill which has proven links to performance and success. And then we'll move on to the importance of understanding our four types of strengths and weaknesses – yes, *four* – and how we can craft a unique career that allows us to play to our best strengths.

As with every other chapter in this book, remember that I don't base my recommendations on speculation or guesswork about what

If hard work alone can't get you to the top, what can?

helps people to succeed. I base my advice on evidence, on published research. This is about the science of winning the race.

Getting to grips with organizational savvy

How good are you at getting your way at work? Here's a test of your organizational savvy. Read the 18 statements below and rate the extent to which you agree or disagree with each one, using the following scale:

1 = strongly disagree
2 = disagree
3 = slightly disagree
4 = neither agree nor disagree
5 = slightly agree
6 = agree
7 = strongly agree

Work your way through the statements fairly swiftly. Pop down a score that reflects your gut instinct. And then I'll explain what it all means afterwards.

	Your score
1. I am able to make most people feel comfortable and at ease around me.	
2. I am able to communicate easily and effectively with others.	
3. It is easy for me to develop good rapport with most people.	

	Your score
4. I understand people very well.	
5. I am good at building relationships with influential people at work.	
6. I am particularly good at sensing the motivation and hidden agendas of others.	
7. When communicating with others, I try to be genuine in what I say and do.	
8. At work, I know a lot of important people and am well connected.	
9. I spend a lot of time at work developing connections with others.	
10. I am good at getting people to like me.	
11. I have developed a large network of colleagues and associates at work who I can call on for support when I really need to get things done.	
12. It is important that people believe I am sincere in what I say or do.	
13. I try to show a genuine interest in other people.	
14. I am good at using my connections and network to make things happen at work.	
15. I have good intuition or savvy about how to present myself to others.	
16. I always seem to instinctively know the right things to say or do to influence others.	
17. I pay close attention to people's facial expressions.	
18. I spend a lot of time and effort at work networking with others.	

Now total up all of your scores in the right-hand column. You should have a score of between 18 and 126. You may want to write your total down; we'll look at what it means shortly.

The 18 statements come from a test developed by Gerald Ferris, a professor of management and psychology at Florida State University. The questionnaire measures a skill which I call "organizational savvy", although others have called it "interpersonal style", "political finesse" or "street smarts". But what we call it matters less than what it measures. Researchers such as Ferris and his colleagues define it as "the ability to effectively understand others at work, and to use such knowledge to influence others to act in ways that enhance one's personal and/or organizational objectives."[1]

In other words, organizational savvy means being able to understand, build and use relationships in order to achieve goals. People with organizational savvy comprehend that hard work and good ideas alone are rarely enough to guarantee success – it often takes the unabashed support or sponsorship of teammates, bosses and colleagues from other departments to get things done.

Individuals with organizational savvy are interpersonal chameleons who can coax or command, inspire or influence colleagues, depending on the needs of different situations. They build friendships, coalitions and alliances in order to secure backing and resources for their projects; they trade favours and take the time to bring others on board. And they do so in ways that are honest, sincere and in the best interests of the team or wider organization – or at least in ways that appear to be genuine rather than self-serving or manipulative.

Organizational savvy means being able to understand, build and use relationships in order to achieve goals.

Multiple studies from across the world tell us that organizational savvy matters. In one survey conducted in Australia, for instance, psychologist Assaf Semadar and his colleagues persuaded the human resources department of a car manufacturing business to give them information about the annual performance evaluations of 136 managers. Asking the managers to complete a battery of psychological tests, the research team found clear evidence that managers who had high levels of organizational savvy were also the most likely to be rated as being "top achievers". In fact, organizational savvy was a better predictor of performance than even the managers' levels of emotional intelligence – that construct which not so many years ago was touted as the key to success in life, work and everything.[2]

A separate American study found that organizational savvy helped to protect employees from emotional burnout.[3] And, as a final example, a third investigation conducted in China observed that employees who scored highly on organizational savvy were not only rated by their supervisors as the most valuable but also recommended for more rewards from their bosses too.[4]

Taking all of these studies together, we know that organizational savvy helps people in countries all over the world to succeed.[5] And here's the good news: while certain hotshots may naturally start out with a bit more of it, it's ultimately a skill that can be shaped, developed and honed.

Honing your organizational savvy

So how did you score on the organizational savvy questionnaire? We can't say for certain what an average score is – as the different studies have been conducted in totally diverse groups ranging from veteran managers in Germany to financial analysts in the Midwest United States. But the average score is typically in the region of 95 to 99.

However, the purpose of the questionnaire isn't so much to tell you whether you're above average, below average or average. The point is that your current score represents where you are *now*. Just because you may score at around the average mark doesn't mean you should rest on your laurels. Think of it this way: if you're average, that means that out of 20 colleagues, you probably have nine or 10 who are better than you and more likely to get promoted. That's not really being a winner, is it? And even if you're already somewhat above average, what's got you to this point in your career may not get you much further unless you can hone your organizational savvy.

I often ask individuals that I'm coaching to complete the organizational savvy questionnaire as a diagnostic test, as a way for me to investigate their skills and challenges better. For instance, I recently worked with an executive at a high street retailer of men's and women's clothing, whom I'll call Karen. A forthright woman on the cusp of her 50th year with spiky tufts of silver-blonde hair and a tendency to speak at machine-gun pace, she sought me out because she was frustrated that her upward progress within the company seemed to have run out of steam.

When I met her, she was a regional managing director in charge of eight stores, including two prestigious flagship stores; she was responsible for over 40 managers and deputy managers and nearly 150 employees under them.

She was hungry to take the next step up to become a divisional director in charge of 30 stores and close to a thousand employees. But she had been stuck in her current role for nearly six years and seen other, sometimes younger, colleagues vault ahead of her.

Karen completed the organizational savvy questionnaire and achieved a score of 108. She was already above average. But we then scrutinized the individual statements on which she had scored lowest. She already either agreed or strongly agreed with many of the statements, but she fell down on a few others.

For example, she only gave herself a "4" on "I am good at building relationships with influential people at work". She already networked a lot with other regional managing directors and many of the buying and merchandizing team back at head office. But she had an epiphany: she could be spending a lot more time with the movers and shakers – the influencers and decision-makers – within the company.

Immediately, we discussed options for remedying that and she decided that she would make it a priority to seek out senior executives whenever she was at head office, which was usually once every few weeks. Rather than waiting to be asked to meet with them, Karen decided that she would find reasons to ask them for time in their diaries. That way, she could find out about the company's strategies and challenges and look for ways she could contribute, and in doing so prove that she was a valuable team player.

Karen also gave herself a lower score on the statement "I am particularly good at sensing the motivation and hidden agendas of others". She said that everyone around her knew exactly what her motivations and agendas were. She frequently spoke her mind when she had ideas or suggestions. When she disagreed with colleagues, she was quick to voice her opinions. In fact, she had sometimes been slated for being too direct, too blunt in her views.

However, she recognized that not all of her colleagues were as open as she was. Just because she didn't have secret motives or hidden agendas didn't mean that others didn't have more clandestine goals and objectives.

At first, Karen didn't know how she could get better at reading the motivations and agendas of others. Eventually, though, she hit upon two ideas. First, she decided that she would spend more time with her good friend Howard, an operations director at head office. She described Howard as someone who was naturally plugged into the power struggles and intrigues within the company. So she hoped that, by spending more time with him, she could appeal to him to guide and mentor her through the political landscape.

Second, she opted to keep track of her colleagues' goals and priorities. In the past, she had focused very firmly on her own targets and the tasks she needed to do to succeed in hitting the objectives that the organization had set for her. However, she started making notes about her senior colleagues' issues, what they were wrestling with and what they seemed to be looking for. Doing so encouraged her to keep their motives and agendas much more at the forefront of her mind.

I last heard from Karen about six months ago. She hadn't been promoted yet but for the first time in years she was confident that she was moving in the right direction and that a promotion would be forthcoming.

Developing your organizational savvy

So which statements did you rate lowest in the organizational savvy questionnaire? You may find that you have more than a handful of statements on which you scored less highly than you would have wished. However, the aim here isn't to work on lots of different actions at once.

I usually recommend to clients I'm coaching to identify a small number – perhaps only three or four actions – to take on initially. Even if there might be many things you *could* work on, choose to do less to begin with. That way, you focus and give yourself a better shot at actually achieving them.

Look at the statements and choose the ones you feel you would *like* to work on most. If you feel that certain actions may be easier or more enjoyable to take on, start with those.

If you're at all stuck for ideas on how to develop your organizational savvy, contemplate some combination of the following:

- Talk through issues with a mentor – either a senior person within the organization or perhaps one outside of it.

- Work with an external coach.

- Role play with colleagues.

- Engage in mental rehearsal.

- Discuss issues and seek advice from trusted colleagues.

- Observe colleagues you consider role models for organizational savvy. What do they say or do that helps them to do well?

Taking your organizational savvy to the next level

The many studies showing the importance of organizational savvy ultimately tell us that career success is only *partly* determined by intelligence and hard work.[6] I mentioned at the start of the chapter that many workers labour under the mistaken belief that hard work and splendid ideas alone are enough to get ahead. But we now know that's not the case.

The new manifesto for success suggests that our performance is judged as much on our relationships – our ability to form them, use them and rally support for projects through them – as on our completion of mere tasks. Because, in my view, organizational savvy is mostly about reading people, figuring out what makes them tick and finding ways to work with people in ways that will benefit *them* as well as us. Simply presenting even a gorgeous idea to our colleagues or proposing that a project is good for the organization often isn't enough; we need to pitch things to people so that they *personally* get something out of it too.

Our performance is judged as much on our relationships as on our completion of mere tasks.

I'm not saying that this state of play is either desirable or healthy. As we've already seen elsewhere in this book, scientific research doesn't tell us what is morally right or wrong – it only tells us the way things are.

I find the organizational savvy questionnaire a really useful tool for helping clients to think about their effectiveness at work. When researcher Gerald Ferris and his colleagues first designed it, they found that the questionnaire actually operates on two levels. Yes, there's the global level, which we discussed above: a high score denotes better-than-average savvy while a lower score suggests that there's a lot of room for growth. But it turns out that the overall skill of organizational savvy is also made up of four sub-skills.

Let's look at each of the sub-skills. Then we can discuss how they can help us to further sharpen our effectiveness and performance at work:

- **Social Astuteness.** Individuals with a high degree of Social Astuteness are typically keen observers of others' behaviour; they interpret other people's body language and listen carefully to not only the words that others use but also their tone of voice and facial expressions. They scrutinize others carefully and pick up on sarcasm, frustration, disappointment and the many subtler feelings that affect their colleagues. You can calculate your Social Astuteness score by adding up the scores you gave statements 4, 6, 15, 16 and 17.

- **Interpersonal Influence.** Individuals with a finely honed apti-
tude for Interpersonal Influence are chameleons when it
comes to wooing others and winning support. They realize
that different people may be motivated by totally different
things; they therefore flex or adapt their influencing styles
depending on whom they're dealing with. For example, one
colleague may like to be dealt with in a brisk, rational
manner but another colleague may need a softer, more sym-
pathetic approach. A further colleague may need to be won
over with praise and flattery or yet another colleague with
a heartfelt plea for help. Work out your Interpersonal Influence score by tallying up the scores you gave statements 1,
2, 3 and 10.

- **Networking Ability.** Another sub-skill of organizational savvy
is the ability to develop effective working relationships and
even friendships with a diverse range of people: peers, subor-
dinates as well as more senior individuals. Individuals with
this sub-skill appreciate that it's vital to obtain backing, intelligence and resources from colleagues in other teams or departments in order to get projects completed successfully. We
already discussed networking or reaching out *outside* of your
organization in Chapter 4: Winning the Job, but now we're
talking about networking *within* your organization. You can
work out your Networking Ability score by adding together
your scores from statements 5, 8, 9, 11, 14 and 18.

- **Demonstrable Sincerity.** Individuals who are accomplished at
this sub-skill come across as sincere, honourable and possess-
ing high levels of integrity. They are – or at least appear to
be – honest and open. This is a crucial sub-skill, because
people who are low on Demonstrable Sincerity could come
across as self-serving, bullying or manipulative. It's not enough
to have good intentions unless people can *see* that you have
good intentions. Ultimately, it's a matter of trust: do those in
your community trust you? To figure out your score for

Demonstrable Sincerity, add together your individual scores from statements 7, 12 and 13.

To get an idea of where your relative strengths and weak spots may be, another way of using the organizational savvy questionnaire is to compare your sub-skill scores with those of others.

	Average score	Your score
Social Astuteness	27	
Interpersonal Influence	21	
Networking Ability	32	
Demonstrable Sincerity	16	

How do your scores stack up against the average scores for each of the four sub-skills? Are you particularly low on any of them? If so, that should give you some clues as to where to focus your time and efforts. Or, even if you're average or above average on some of them, which are your relative weak spots?

Several months ago I coached a square-jawed executive in the food and drinks industry by the name of Bryce. A perpetually polo-shirt-clad American who had lived in the UK for nearly a decade, his desk was festooned with business awards that he and his team had won. He scored fairly highly on two of the sub-skills but manifestly lower on the Demonstrable Sincerity sub-skill.

At first, he disputed the scores and took offence at the implication that he may have anything but honourable intentions. But I told him that I wasn't trying to trick him. After all, we were scrutinizing the ratings that he himself had assigned to the statements.

Looking again at the Demonstrable Sincerity statements (numbered 7, 12 and 13), Bryce tried to work out why he had given himself lower scores. He decided that it wasn't that he was calculating and trying to be manipulative – it was just that making a good impression and ensuring that he seemed genuine wasn't something he had ever considered much.

In order to tackle statements 7 ("When communicating with others, I try to be genuine in what I say and do") and 12 ("It is important that people believe I am sincere in what I say or do"), Bryce resolved that he would try to be more transparent about his reasons for wanting to pursue projects.

And in response to statement 13 ("I try to show a genuine interest in other people"), he decided to make it a higher priority to demonstrate a greater interest in his colleagues by asking them more questions. To avoid the slightest chance that other people might find him manipulative or conniving, he was determined to work harder at discovering their issues, problems and priorities.

Bryce also scored a little lower on the sub-skill of Networking Ability. He said that he had reservations about networking which were probably tied up with his difficulties with Demonstrable Sincerity. He didn't want anyone to think that he was striking up relationships purely to accrue benefits to his career.

I told him that was a valid concern and one which many people shared. However, I suggested that he could take a fresh approach: he could think about developing relationships with a wider range of people in order to help *them* out. If he ended up being on friendlier terms with them or even making a few more genuine buddies, that would be an added bonus rather than his sole reason for reaching out.

> ### Keeping organizational savvy at the forefront of your mind
>
> If you're serious about wanting to win the race that is your career, you may wish to take a more in-depth look at where your sub-skill scores are lowest. Clearly, not everyone has access to a professional coach. However, most of us have friends in whom we can confide.
>
> So ask one or more of your close friends for help. Your confidant could be someone within your organization, possibly an ex-colleague you still respect or just a sensible person that you trust.
>
> Tell your confidants what you know about the research behind organizational savvy and then discuss where your sub-skill scores are lowest. Read the individual statements that make up each sub-skill and brainstorm ideas for how you can improve.
>
> Don't expect effortless answers. If it were easy, everyone would already be doing it. But remember the research we covered in Chapter 1 telling us that most skills are amenable to improvement: you *can* change, grow and develop your skills so long as you're willing to put in the work.

Playing to your strengths

Time to switch gears now for a change of topic. Let's move on to the second half of the jigsaw puzzle of skills and attitudes that allows people to win the race.

Imagine for a moment that a person you've never met before – a friend of a friend – wants to know who you are and what you are like as a human being. However, that person only needs to find out

a little about you so asks you to list exactly five activities you do
or skills you have that demonstrate who you are. What five activities or skills of importance to you would you list?

When I answered the Personally Expressive Activities Questionnaire for myself, my five skills/activities were:

- Listening and chatting to people.

- Being organized, disciplined and systematic.

- Telling people what to do.

- Being involved in sports, physical exercise, fitness, health and
  nutrition.

- Writing.

You'll see from my list that it isn't restricted to skills and activities
relating only to my work as a business psychologist. These are just
things that define who I am. Take writing, for example. I've always
enjoyed writing for its own sake. I was nine years old when I started
keeping a daily diary. I used to write short stories for fun when I
was growing up too. When I was at university studying psychology
as an undergraduate, I used to research and write extra essays
when I found topics interesting. And even today, I write a couple
of blogs that have nothing to do with my work as a business psychologist – one on comic books and another on ice skating.

So how would you answer the question? What would your
answers be?

You'll get more out of this chapter if you take a few moments to
answer the question rather than rushing on ahead. So here's your
chance to list five activities or skills that you believe are important and
describe who you are. I'm not going to hold you to this initial list, so
jot down the first five aptitudes or activities that come to mind:

■

■

■

■

■

This single-question questionnaire, known as the Personally Expressive Activities Questionnaire, was developed by researcher Alan Waterman at the College of New Jersey to suss out what helps to keep people motivated, interested and satisfied in life.[7] Essentially, research tells us that the more of these valued skills or activities we can use in our jobs, the more likely we are to feel stoked up and satisfied by our work.

It makes sense that being able to focus on what we're good at should make us feel good too, right? When we exercise our strengths and direct our energies on activities of interest to us, we feel motivated and get better results than other people who may be doing the same kind of work. We feel capable, upbeat and confident.

Conversely, when we have to use skills that are underdeveloped, we get worse results than others. And that could make us feel disappointed, self-doubting and stupid.

When we exercise our strengths, we feel motivated and get better results.

Speaking from personal experience, I can definitely attest to the joy and fulfilment of being able to exercise my strengths in my work. Because that's definitely not how things started out initially.

My first job wasn't a great fit for me. After completing my training as a sport and exercise psychologist, I went to work for a large management consulting firm mainly because it sounded prestigious and the salary was nearly double what I could have earned as a trainee psychologist. I worked with clients mainly building spreadsheets to analyze how they could reduce costs and bump up profits. I spent more than 80 per cent of my time staring at a computer monitor and probably less than 10 per cent of the time with people on activities such as interviewing clients (listening) and running workshops (telling people what to do).

At least I could mostly organize my own work (being organized), but as I was only spending a fraction of my time exercising my other strengths, I never really enjoyed the work. I was reasonably competent at building spreadsheets but, boy, did the days drag on. I simply didn't have the drive to hone that skill and become the kind of business analyst and consultant that the job required. And so, despite the fact that the pay and benefits were good, I decided to look for a better job after only two years.

My next job was a much better fit. Joining a firm of business psychologists, I got to spend a lot of my time interviewing clients (listening). I also got the chance to do a fair amount of one-on-one coaching as well as running instructional workshops (telling people what to do). And I was still given a lot of say in how I managed my work and my time (being organized).

I still wasn't involved in sports, health and fitness. And I didn't get much opportunity to write at work. But I was applying three out of my five key strengths perhaps 60 to 70 per cent of the time.

As I moved into another job and eventually quit to set up my own business, I started writing magazine articles and then books as part of my work (writing). And so we get to the present day.

Currently, I don't get much opportunity to involve myself in sports, health and fitness in my work – it's not something that my corporate clients really require of me. But over the years and after successive job changes, I now get the chance to use my main strengths around 80 to 90 per cent of the time. So I'm happy – really delighted – with the work that I do.

So how about you and your career? How many of your top-five skills or valued activities do you get to use in your day-to-day work?

The link between strengths and success

In the past decade or so, proliferating numbers of psychologists, business school professors and other researchers have explored the roles that people's personal strengths play in their lives. And the lessons are clear. Researchers such as professors Martin Seligman at the University of Pennsylvania and the late Christopher Peterson at the University of Michigan in Ann Arbor have found that people who use a greater proportion of their strengths at work feel more engaged, switched on and alive.[8] They relish the challenges they encounter and get an upwelling of satisfaction from learning new things. They enjoy their work *and* work harder. And, as you might expect, they also tend to be more successful too – they get promoted more quickly, earn more money and generally make better progress towards their goals.[9]

Does any of that sound interesting at all?

I'm coaching a serial entrepreneur called Jamie at the moment. A towering Irishman in his late 30s with a thundering baritone and a predilection for telling bawdy jokes, he has already successfully set up and sold a multimillion-pound business and is in the midst of running a second company. He listed his five as:

- Thinking about money and how to make it.

- Selling, pitching and sweet-talking.

- Feeling in charge and being the boss of whatever I do.

- Curiosity and tinkering (i.e. coming up with ideas, changing things and seeing how to improve stuff).

- Working with others in teams and groups (rather than working by myself).

Throughout his 20s, Jamie had a tolerably successful career in a half-dozen sales roles, which included selling advertising for a magazine publisher, warranties for an engineering company and computer hardware to businesses. While he did well enough at each company, he certainly wasn't a top salesperson on the fast track to success either.

As the years passed, he became increasingly weary of selling things for other people. So, shortly after his 31st birthday, he talked two ex-colleagues into starting up a business with him: a computing and technology solutions consultancy.

The company exploded in size almost immediately. The company hit more than a million pounds in sales within just 14 months. Less than three years later, Jamie and his partners received an offer from a larger competitor to buy them out. And, two years after that, Jamie left the company on amicable terms with a substantial seven-figure sum in his pocket for his efforts.

Why? What was responsible for his success? In talking about his empire-building success, Jamie is quick to point out that he felt thoroughly worn down at times. He struggled to hire the right people to cope with the growth and made some nearly disastrous decisions along the way. He also had many personal low points when he felt that the business was putting too much of a strain on his life, relationships and even health.

But he sees his success as primarily to do with the fact that he felt much more fired up and fulfilled as an entrepreneur building his own business than he had ever felt as a sales executive selling products and services for others. Growing his business, figuring out what worked and didn't work and nurturing his own team tested and challenged him so much more than simply selling had ever done. He had come alive in using the full array of his strengths to run his own business.

Of course, there are many factors that govern whether any individual will be successful or not. Intelligence, creativity and hard work all contribute to the picture, as do skills such as organizational savvy. External factors such as political and economic conditions, market trends and even dumb luck also play a part. But so too does being able to use our strengths and feeling fulfilled rather than worn down by our work.

The single question that I asked in the previous section (about your five activities or skills of importance) is only a very basic way of exploring your strengths – a quick glance at the tip of the iceberg. So what's a better way to discover the full range of your assets? And, once you've identified your strengths, how can you carve out a career that will allow you to be not only happier but also more successful?

The role of hard work

In the last few years, there's been a popular view that nearly anyone can become an expert at anything – music, sport, chess, writing, business, whatever – simply through enough hard work. In the bestselling 2008 book *Outliers*, the writer Malcolm Gladwell told the stories of many successful individuals – ranging from Bill Gates to the Beatles – who had succeeded through their sheer hard work, through the accumulation of thousands and thousands of hours of practice.[10]

It's a beguiling notion because it suggests that anyone can turn any skill into a strength with enough hard work. The idea is particularly comforting because it tells us that everyone has a shot and that those who succeed do so only because they deserved it – they worked harder than the rest.

Unfortunately, the latest research tells us that this view is wrong. *Totally* wrong.

The evidence comes from a 2013 paper published in a top scientific journal, *Intelligence*. An international team of psychologists from the UK, the USA and Australia looked at star performers in the fields of music and chess. And their conclusion? Hard work alone is *not* enough to guarantee success.

Looking at the practice diaries of chess grand-masters and their peak ratings (i.e. the highest in the world rankings that they ever achieved), the researchers concluded that only 34 per cent of the differences between the very best and weaker players could be accounted for by hard work alone. For example, the researchers analyzed raw data pertaining to three Hungarian sisters who had been schooled intensively from a young age by their chess-playing father, a chess grandmaster and a bevy of chess teachers.

Judit Polgár achieved a World Chess Federation rating of 2735 in an estimated 59,904 hours of practice – she's the strongest woman chess player in history. However, Judit's older sister, Zsuzsa, attained a rating of only 2577 despite putting in around 79,248 hours of practice. In other words, Judit managed to beat her sister to the top despite having spent a massive 1,344 *fewer* hours (or six years and seven months of eight-hour days, seven days a week) actually playing chess.

The researchers also found similar results amongst pianists and other musicians. Sheer hours of practice only accounted for 29.9

per cent of the difference between the truly outstanding musicians and their less accomplished peers.

The researchers are unreservedly emphatic in their conclusions: "The evidence is quite clear that some people *do* reach an elite level of performance without copious practice, while other people fail to do so *despite* copious practice."[11]

Let's think about this for a bit. Both music and chess are relatively well-defined skills. They don't require physical strength, height or power. So in theory everyone should be able to graft away at them. But the research found that hard work alone only got people so far – about a third of the way, in fact. Something else mattered more.

Don't get me wrong. I'm not saying that hard work doesn't make a difference. Cast your mind back to Chapter 1: Developing a Winning Outlook and you'll recall that research into the growth mind-set tells us that improvement is possible in nearly every area of our lives. And these music and chess studies suggest that hard work can take us a third of the way to where we want to be. But sometimes if a skill isn't a natural strength, growth may mean *some* improvement as opposed to unfettered success.

To me, this is verifiable evidence that we need to understand what our natural strengths are. There's no point trying to become a top investment analyst if spreadsheets and numbers aren't your forte or an advertising executive if creativity doesn't come easily. Why waste your time and put in a Herculean effort working at something and trying to make a career of it if your personality, values or inclinations are elsewhere?

What is a "strength" exactly?

So here's the bad news: there's no quick way of ascertaining what your strengths are. I wish I could invite you to complete a straightforward questionnaire which could ping out an answer about your strengths, but I can't.

For a start, competing groups of researchers have been unable to agree on the best questions to ask for measuring strengths. There are at least a handful of wildly different strengths questionnaires based on conflicting research methodologies. But in my view, none of them does the job perfectly, because human strengths are simply too complex and multifaceted to be categorized by questionnaires alone.

That doesn't mean that we can't work out our strengths. However, it does mean that it will take a bit longer to do so.

Before we attempt to identify your particular advantages, let's chew over in a bit more detail what we actually mean by a "strength". Researchers, such as Alex Linley at the Centre for Applied Positive Psychology in the UK, argue that we can categorize our skills, abilities and weaknesses by asking ourselves two questions:[12]

- **"To what extent does an activity energize us?"** Some activities make us feel energized and more positive. Other tasks make us feel drained. For example, I find painting, decorating and fixing things around the house really tiresome and enervating – I gladly hire other people to do them. However, I have plenty of buddies who really enjoy those activities and get a buzz out of them.

- **"What kind of results do we get from the activity?"** Some activities we're already good at, for example I know I'm better than average at public speaking and giving engaging presentations. Other activities we know we're not so good at: I know I'm not very good at soothing and mollifying other people's children, and those who can would make much better nannies and child care providers than me.

That means that we get a two-by-two matrix for all of our skills and talents:

		Acquired Behaviours	Realized Strengths
Quality of your results	Good		
	Bad	Genuine Weaknesses	Unrealized Strengths

| | Negative | Positive |

Energy that you gain from exercising the skill

The four categories of skills and abilities are as follows:

- **Realized Strengths.** These are skills that both energize us and currently also give us good results. So we enjoy using these strengths *and* know that we perform them well. When I say that we *enjoy* using our strengths, some people report that they feel engaged and alive, while others say that they find such activities meaningful or perhaps that they get a rewarding sense of challenge from them. The more we can apply our Realized Strengths both at work and in our personal lives outside of work, the more we can feel motivated and invigorated. We may also be most likely to succeed when we can play to these truest strengths too.

- **Unrealized Strengths.** These are skills that we enjoy using or find rewarding to do but which currently may not give us terribly good results. For example, I take great delight in singing but I've been told by family and friends that I'm not very tuneful! We may not be able to exercise our Unrealized Strengths – perhaps owing to our personal circumstances or work situations – but we certainly derive satisfaction and pleasure when we do get to use them. In order to get better results, we would need training and practice, although there's still no guarantee that we could get good enough to base a career upon these skills.

- **Acquired Behaviours.** I use this term to describe the skills that we have learnt over time to do well in spite of the fact that we may derive little pleasure or energy from them. Consider a client I worked with who was a proficient public speaker. She was repeatedly praised by colleagues for her engaging, witty presentations. However, she didn't appreciate having to write and rewrite her material. She found it tiring to practise her presentations. And she felt very nervous when presenting. Even though she had over the years learnt to become a lively public speaker, it was definitely a hard-won Acquired Behaviour for her rather than a skill she enjoyed exercising. The advice from the experts: the more we can minimize the amount of Acquired Behaviours we have to perform in our lives, the more fulfilled and satisfied we may feel.

- **Genuine Weaknesses.** Performing these activities not only saps our energy and motivation; it also leads to worse-than-average results. This is the worst of both worlds: we're not very good at the skill and we also lack the drive to improve at it. Being forced to work on these tasks for long would be both demoralizing and unproductive. So the key to having a happier and more successful life is to find ways to get around these Genuine Weaknesses. For example, one route may be to find partners who can do these tasks for us – perhaps in exchange for our doing some of the tasks that they dislike or aren't very good at. Or we could try to seek out different jobs or even entirely new professions that don't require us to spend so much time on our shortcomings.

I like this four-way categorization because it helps us to distinguish between the various types of things we're good at. For instance, I can build a better spreadsheet than many people I know because I spent most of two years learning how to use Excel in my first job. However, I get only a tiny amount of gratification from it and it feels like hard work. Consequently, working with spreadsheets is an Acquired Behaviour for me.

In contrast, an ex-colleague and friend of mine called Johnson gets a major kick out of building spreadsheets. In fact, when we worked together at the same firm, he taught himself how to manipulate Visual Basic programming language in his spare time, for fun. Working with spreadsheets is a Realized Strength, a genuine passion *and* skill for him.

Anyway, that's enough of the theory. Let's bring things closer to home.

Identifying your own strengths

Earlier in this chapter, I asked you to list five skills and activities that are important to you and represent who you are. But clearly most of us have many, many more skills and areas of interest. So what are yours?

There are many assorted ways of investigating our strengths; different people like using different techniques, so here I'll present three contrasting approaches from which you can choose. I'd suggest using at least a couple of them in order to get different perspectives on your strengths. However, for the most in-depth insight into yourself, you could also use all three.

Exploring your own strengths

When in life do you remember feeling that you were firing on all cylinders – when you were working hard but having a magnificent time of things?

One way of looking at your strengths is to bring to mind specific occasions when you felt particularly motivated and stimulated. These may be from your professional or personal life, your leisure activities, for example. You might have lost track of time because you were so engrossed in what you were doing; you were probably proud of the results you achieved too.

Think about a handful – perhaps between two and five – of these highlights in your life. For each one, write a paragraph about your circumstances to prompt yourself over when it occurred and what you were doing.

Once you've written briefly about each and reminded yourself what happened, simply list the strengths that you felt you displayed in each. Finally, when you've listed all of the strengths you exhibited across your different highlights, look back at your lists to look for patterns. What were the *key* strengths, the so-called signature strengths, which typify your life's best moments?

Using this first exercise may help you in particular to spot some of your Realized and Unrealized Strengths. Remember that our Realized Strengths are the ones which we both enjoy using and from which we get good results. Our Unrealized Strengths give us pleasure but perhaps not such marvellous results because we haven't honed and developed them yet.

If you liked that first exercise, you could also have a go at its opposite too. Think back to a handful of times in your life when you were working hard but felt demoralized, deflated or out of your depth. Why? What skills or behaviours were you being forced to use at the time?

Our Realized Strengths are the ones which we both enjoy using and from which we get good results.

Don't dwell on the circumstances too long – the aim here isn't to circle the drain and make yourself relive them all over again. But by briefly revisiting a couple of negative situations in your life, can you spot any Genuine Weaknesses? And, if so, how could you orchestrate your work and life in order to avoid falling into the same trap again?

Delving into our strengths requires equal portions of rational evaluation and gut feel. We can get objective indicators about the quality of our work from our bosses' reports, our colleagues' comments as well as our own dispassionate observations of how we stack up against others.

But we have to trust our instincts and emotions too. Only we can truly know how much energy we derive from an activity – whether it's fun or fatiguing.

Getting a second opinion on your strengths

A different approach to looking at your strengths is to seek the opinions of people in your life – not just work colleagues but also friends and family who know you well. If you want to take a systematic approach, you could send out an email inviting people's comments along the lines of the following:

I'm currently trying to understand my profile of strengths better so that I can make better career decisions. As someone whose opinion I value, I'd really appreciate your honest answers.

What do you think my strengths are? Feel free to define "strength" in any way you like. If you had to say that I was good at five things, what would you say those things were?

Alternatively, you could wait until you caught up with friends over the telephone or in person to chat about it more informally. But try to get as many perspectives from as many diverse areas of your life as you can. Your current colleagues will only tend to know the strengths you get to demonstrate in your current job; previous colleagues may have entirely different perspectives. And family members or friends from way back may be able to comment on other strengths that you may not have exercised for some time.

Asking your colleagues, friends and family for their comments on your strengths will tend to point out the things that you're good at, the behaviours you exhibit that get good results. But remember that there are two types of skills that get good results. Realized Strengths both give us pleasure and above-average results. Acquired Behaviours also may lead to better-than-average results but may be draining to perform.

The people in your life often won't be able to tell the difference between the two. Most onlookers will applaud the good results you get without knowing the possible sacrifices you have to make in order to execute Acquired Behaviours.

Delving even further into your strengths

This final strengths exercise is the most time-consuming but also the most comprehensive of the three in this chapter. Essentially, you need to figure out a chronology of everything you've done in your life. It's like writing a mini-memoir of your entire life from your late teens to the present day.

You'll especially appreciate this exercise if you're the kind of person who enjoys writing a lot – writing a journal, making to-do lists and so on. But not everyone finds it easy to review their lives in such a diligent and thorough manner, so don't beat yourself up if you don't complete this one.

Taking an in-depth look at your strengths

Try looking at your strengths by reviewing the triumphs and successes you've experienced on a year-by-year basis throughout your life. Here's how:

- Start by working out the year you were 18 years old. Write the year down at the top of a sheet of paper.

- Next, write a few bullet points on the page about what you did that year. Where were you living? What were you doing? List everything work-related, such as paid jobs, as well as voluntary work. And then include some notes on your leisure activities too.

- Then think about your highlights for that year. What did you enjoy and get the biggest buzz from? What personal or professional projects made you feel in control, confident or exhilarated?

- Finally, write down the skills – the strengths – you deployed during those projects that made you feel so good.

Once you've done all of that, you can write the next year at the top of another sheet of paper and then repeat for the year you were 19, and then 20, 21 and so on. Obviously, if you're only in your early 20s, this exercise will take less time than if you are in your 50s or 60s!

A good place to start would be the latest version of your CV for dates of various jobs. Take a look back at old diaries, journals, emails and letters, too, if it helps.

You don't have to do this exercise in one sitting. Most clients take their time with it, working their way through their life histories perhaps a few years at a time. The more carefully you review your personal and professional high points, the more likely you will be to identify your true strengths – both your Realized Strengths as well as your Unrealized Strengths.

This final exercise is particularly useful for helping us to rediscover strengths that we may have forgotten about. Sometimes, people find that their careers almost take on a life of their own; they chase promotions and pay rises even though such rewards sometimes take them away from being able to exercise their strengths. And then they find themselves being trapped into doing things that either bore or drain them.

Choosing the right career path

Great, so now you've discovered your strengths. And we know that people who get to exercise their key strengths on a regular basis feel more fulfilled and satisfied in their work (and lives) than those

People who get to exercise their key strengths on a regular basis feel more fulfilled and satisfied in their work.

who don't. So what next? What does this all mean for your career and life?

To answer such questions, allow me to present you with a little dilemma. Let's say that a friend of yours has come to you for advice about his career. We'll call him Owen.

He tells you that the human resources department at his company asked the senior managers across the business to score everybody's skills on scales of between 1 and 10. A "1" indicates a major short-coming, "5" is average and "10" is an exceptional strength. He just got his own results and isn't sure what to do about them.

Like most of his colleagues, Owen discovered that he has a lot of skills that are fairly average – scoring in the region of 5 or 6. He is competent at communicating in writing, listening to colleagues and asserting himself during team meetings. He plans and manages his time as well as most people and has reasonable research and project management skills. And he has acceptable negotiation and persuasive skills.

He was pleased to discover that he scored 7s and 8s on a couple of skills: he had strengths in problem-solving, data analysis and business modelling. Less happily, he also scored 2s and 3s in areas such as public speaking and delivering customer service.

So now Owen faces a dilemma. He doesn't know what to do next.

Option A would be to find a different role that allowed him to spend more time utilizing his strengths. So that would be a job that focused more on identifying and solving problems by delving into data and creating business models of likely outcomes. And, clearly, it would involve fewer customer service and public-speaking demands. There may be such a role within another department, or perhaps he could try to cajole his manager into changing his job description to match his strengths. But if such opportunities weren't available within his current company, it could mean having to look elsewhere for a totally different job with a totally different organization.

Option B would be to work on his weak spots. Owen explains that both his manager and the human resources department want him to improve specifically on his weaker skills. They want him to volunteer to give more presentations so that he becomes both more comfortable and adept at public speaking. And they would like him to attend several customer service courses so that he can interact with customers more sensitively and effectively.

Doing all of that would help him plug the gaps in his skill set. But Owen doesn't want to have to do more presentations – not because he gets nervous but simply because he finds them a tedious way to pass the time. And he can think of more exciting things to do than spend any more time with customers than he already has to.

So which option would you advise Owen to take? Option A or Option B? Should he look for ways of playing to his strengths or work on shoring up his weaknesses?

Of course, Owen is a made-up person facing a purely hypothetical situation. But it's also an illustration of the real-life conundrum facing many people.

There is an inescapable wave of evidence showing that people who get to exercise their strengths regularly feel more engaged in their work. However, the reality is that most organizations try to get their employees to take Option B – encouraging any square-shaped people to conform to the round-shaped holes that they need.

Organizations don't do this to spite employees deliberately. It's just the way organizations work: they write job descriptions detailing the skills they need and then encourage employees to develop their skills to fit those jobs. It's a rare company that is willing to do the reverse, of tailoring jobs to fit the skills of its people.

Pursuing Option A: Reshaping your work to your strengths

In discussing Owen's fate, I didn't pick Option A and Option B by chance. I refer to Option A because I think that the "A" stands for "autonomy" or for becoming your own career "architect". You take the foundation of your strengths and build your own ideal job on top of it. Rather than trying to compete with the rest of the crowd, why not carve out your own niche where you can reign supreme?

But when it comes to choosing between Option A and Option B, there's no single answer that is right for everyone. Yes, Option A tends to make people happier and more contented in their work and it's the path I've worked with many clients on achieving. So rather than trying to force themselves into the mould that their organizations required of them, they decided to look for opportunities that would allow them to build on their strengths instead.

Some decided to cast around for new jobs elsewhere or decided to retrain so that they could enter entirely new professions. A few chose to set up their own businesses so that they could do things entirely their own way.

That doesn't mean, though, that success and happiness can come only from quitting your job to go elsewhere. Some people keen to exercise their strengths manage to negotiate different roles within their existing companies. Others find that they can get greater satisfaction simply by making a more determined effort to pursue projects that interest and excite them. And tweaking your current role is a whole lot less risky than ditching your job for something entirely new.

I worked with one client – a lean, boyishly bombastic 50-something called Alan – who felt very stuck in his career and life. He had worked his way up to becoming a fairly senior level healthcare executive. He had responsibility and managed a large team and budget, but he felt that he was little more than a medium-sized cog within a monstrous machine. He felt utterly bored and frustrated and said that he had done so for quite a few years.

> Tweaking your current role is a whole lot less risky than ditching your job for something entirely new.

While completing the chronological strengths exercise (see the "Taking an in-depth look at your strengths" box on page 192), Alan immediately realized that some of his most cherished jobs from way, way back in his career had allowed him to use his hands. One of his favourite memories from a summer job he took while at university had involved his working on a farm. He had dug ditches, mucked out stables, fixed fences and done all manner of manual tasks.

Working with his hands wasn't really an option in his day job for a senior executive such as himself. But the simple realization that he missed the satisfaction of fixing things and literally getting his hands dirty encouraged him to find new hobbies outside of his work to act as a pressure valve for the frustrations of his day job.

Alan also learnt that several of his favourite projects in the past had involved running focus groups to gather the opinions of hospital patients, nurses, doctors and other stakeholders. As a senior manager, he now wasn't expected to do that kind of work. However, he decided that it could still be a useful for him to meet with stakeholders occasionally, partly because it would help to remind him who his ultimate customers were and partly because he would simply enjoy it.

There were many things he couldn't change. He still had to attend myriad internal meetings. He still had to pore over budgets with his finance managers. He still had dozens of forms to complete and reports to write every week. However, making several relatively small adjustments in what he did and how he spent his time – not just running more focus groups but also volunteering to chair more inter-departmental work groups, for example – helped him to feel considerably more rewarded by his work rather than run down by it.

Pursuing a different Option A route: Looking elsewhere

But what if you can't get what you're looking for in your current job? What if you still can't find the kinds of assignments you relish doing? If you are satisfied that you have made your best efforts to pursue more interesting work but are still feeling stymied and stifled, perhaps it really is time to look for a new job elsewhere.

Last year, for instance, I met a 40-something sales director called Simone. A guarded woman who offered only the lightest of hand-shakes, she was one of several sales directors managing teams of salespeople who sold advertising space both within magazines and on websites. I had been brought in by the managing director of the business to run a leadership and team-building programme for around a dozen executives as the business was struggling – as were many of its competitors – in a weak economy.

While most of the executives worked to come up with ways of working together more effectively to boost the business, Simone sought me out for a private discussion and confided that she had had enough. She explained that the company had a tough sales culture with an unrelenting focus on performance. Her sales team had not only annual, quarterly and monthly targets but weekly and even daily targets to achieve.

In the past year alone, she had recruited over a dozen young, eager salespeople only to fire most of them within mere months when they were unable to hit their targets. The merciless pace of firing and re-hiring was taking an emotional toll on Simone. She knew that she wanted out.

As part of our exploration of her options, she mapped out her strengths and spotted that she had a penchant for coaching and nurturing people – something which was increasingly impossible in her existing role given the weak economy and the company's drive for instant results.

As a sales professional, Simone had little problem with networking, so swiftly reached out to the people she knew. On each occasion, she adroitly asked for advice and recommendations: what kind of role would suit her strengths?

She secured an introduction to one manager who worked within the human resources department of a huge accountancy firm. The firm was looking to grow its team of internal coaches. Their remit: to help accountants make the transition from doing technical work to building relationships with clients and selling more effectively. And while the firm was equally interested in results, it focused on timeframes of years rather than mere months.

It was the perfect match for her strengths. While Simone knew little about accounting, the depth of her experience in sales and business development combined with her passion for developing others gave her a real edge. Needless to say, when the accounting firm offered her a job, she gladly accepted it.

Taking Option B: Choosing to forge on in spite of your weaknesses

While individuals like Alan and Simone decided to find their own, autonomous Option A paths, I've also coached people who chose to take the Option B route. They were willing to shape themselves to fit the organization's needs. Rather than looking for ways to apply their unique strengths, some people are ready to work on their weaknesses even though they understand the mental costs of doing so.

Some people are ready to work on their weaknesses even though they understand the mental costs of doing so.

Some of these individuals didn't feel that their organizations or bosses would allow them to renegotiate the nature of their work. Others had their own reasons – sometimes financial pressures, sheer ambition, desire for status and so on – that made them determined to improve upon their weak spots.

It wasn't always easy for them to attain the levels of skills that their bosses required of them. Not all of them succeeded, but some did.

So what about you? Which path have you been following in your career so far? Reflect for a moment on your own career and the choices you've made over the years. Option A: have you tried to find jobs that fit your profile of skills? Or Option B: have you been guided by your organization and tried to develop the skills that you needed to fit your jobs?

Whether you followed Option A or Option B in the past doesn't matter. Because what's done is done. Your history can't be rewritten.

The more important point here is that it's time to take control of your future. Course-correct and set your sights on Option A or, if you have already been doing so, decide to pursue it even more aggressively. This isn't just about *feeling* happier and more satisfied in your work. Remember that the research suggests that playing to our strengths allows us to become objectively more successful too.

Compensating for Genuine Weaknesses

So far I've talked a lot about how using our strengths can make us both feel more fulfilled and get better results. But let me finish this section with a short note about our weaknesses.

In an *ideal* world, we'd never have to do any tasks that relied upon any of our Genuine Weaknesses. But, of course, we live in the real world. So what can we do when our jobs require us to do assignments that both drain us and lead to less-than-great results? Here are three tactics for managing our weaknesses:

- **Tackle the task using a Realized Strength.** Just because *many* people may do a task a certain way doesn't mean that you have to. Say you work in sales and most of your fellow salespeople sell by charming or duping customers. If you don't find that style of selling works for you, you could try to be perhaps a more analytical salesperson – by presenting well-made, rational arguments about the benefits of your product. Get creative and think about how to apply one of your Realized Strengths to the same task.

- **Find a colleague with complementary strengths.** Bosses do this all of the time – they hire people who can do the stuff they can't or prefer not to do themselves. But colleagues often trade work informally with peers who have complementary strengths too. For example, I know of two

(*Continued*)

executives working in event management who go to each other for different tasks. Sandrine goes to Aaron when she needs help brainstorming ideas – she knows that she isn't the most creative person in the world. But Aaron admits that he struggles to stay organized and get involved in detail, so he seeks out Sandrine to check his project plans and proofread proposal documents before they go out to clients. Who could appreciate and be good at tasks that you don't enjoy and aren't so good at?

- **Reshape your work role.** Try renegotiating what you are required to do in your job. You may not be able to do away with all of the parts of your job that you don't enjoy. But even handing off one or two duties or having to perform them a little less frequently may allow you to savour the rest of your work more – and perform more strongly a greater proportion of the time.

So there we have three options that may help you to reduce your reliance on shortcomings and to play more frequently to your strengths. But what if you've explored all three options and none of them come to fruition – and you're still stuck doing the tasks you hate?

A fourth option is to develop the weak spot – the skill that you don't enjoy – until it is *good enough*. So you may have to go on a training course, read about the topic, shadow a colleague or spend more time working on the skill until you can perform it at least adequately.

I'm not suggesting that you have to become the best in the team at the task – just that you may need to work at it until the people around you don't really notice that it's a failing any more. This is about taking your skill level from a 2 out of 10 to a 4 or 5 out of

10. Trying to develop your skill any further may swallow up too much time and effort – if it's even possible at all. And then, in the longer term, you can look for a next career move that will allow you to reshape your role even further to suit your strengths.

Bringing everything together to win the race

We began this chapter by exploring research showing that individuals who possess more organizational savvy tend to perform better. You'll remember that organizational savvy comprises four sub-skills including Interpersonal Influence (being able to use different influencing styles with different folks) and Networking Ability (building working relationships with a larger number of people).

I recently worked alongside a manager in the exhibitions industry by the name of Wendell who was an excellent example of how organizational savvy can help a person to thrive. Despite having joined the business only four years ago as an entry-level account executive, he had already reached a senior position as an accounts director. His first promotion came less than a year into the job; the next was still relatively fast, at 18 months. As a late 20-something, he was nearly a decade younger than several of his fellow account directors.

Despite having the threatening build of a heavyweight boxer, Wendell is prone to bouts of spontaneous grinning that make him fantastic company. One day over dim sum in a Chinese restaurant, he told me that the next jump up the career ladder to becoming a client director probably wasn't far off. However, he admitted that he was far from the most intelligent person in the business.

Neither was he the most technically brilliant individual. He also confessed that he didn't put in as many hours as many of his colleagues – including many of the people that he had overtaken on his way up the hierarchy.

So what had helped him to make such heady progress?

Wendell explained that he had a wonderful relationship with his boss – the two of them got on well both at work and outside of it. He said that he also made an effort to chat to clients – to get to know them socially as well as professionally. He bantered and had fun with them; he collected relationships as voraciously as some people hoard matchbooks or expensive shoes.

I told him about the research showing that Interpersonal Influence and Networking Ability were two core sub-skills related to success. He hadn't encountered the notion of organizational savvy before, but he nodded and said that it made sense. Sure, he wasn't the best or hardest worker in the firm, but he was certainly one of the most liked, both by his colleagues and by his clients. Colleagues *enjoyed* working with him. Clients *wanted* to work with him.

Ultimately, people like him. And that's down to his social skill.

Is that fair? Some would say no. But I say yes. Emphatically yes. Social skill is still a *skill*; it's as much of a skill as being good at public speaking, using Photoshop or using financial accounts.

And social skill is transferable to any job. Whether you're working on an oilrig or a trading floor, it helps to be able to understand and get on with people. That's all organizational savvy really is. It's about getting to know people so that they know you *and like you*. Once people know you and like you, it would be a surprise if they *didn't* want to help you out in your career.

We also saw in this chapter that understanding our strengths and then seeking greater Option A career autonomy by changing the nature of our work helps people to both feel more fulfilled *and* perform more successfully. But what if you feel that organizational savvy – and particularly the skills of networking and influencing – are *not* strengths of yours and perhaps even Genuine Weaknesses?

To answer the question, allow me to take you back for a moment to the section "Improving your influence: Adopting both/and thinking", which started on page 65 in Chapter 2: Winning the Argument. I suggested back there that the real world doesn't always fit into nice compartments. Rather than allowing us to think in terms of either/or, we have to get comfortable with the messy reality of both/and thinking. So my recommendation to most people is that they should work on *both* their organizational savvy *and* the Option A career autonomy tactics.

Studies conclusively show that people with better organizational savvy skills get a bump in their effectiveness and performance. There are few jobs that don't benefit from having better relationships with more of the people around us. So even if networking and influencing people should prove to be amongst your Genuine Weaknesses, I'd say that they are important enough that they still need to be worked on.

> There are few jobs that don't benefit from having better relationships with more of the people around us.

At the same time, you can seek more career autonomy by thinking about ways to reduce the extent to which you have to depend upon your other weaknesses – just not networking and influencing people!

Life sometimes means doing things that we don't want to do. And if you truly yearn to win the race at work, that may mean having to augment your organizational savvy a bit even though it may not be your first preference.

Having said that, though, no one can force you to develop skills against your will. The choice is entirely yours. It all comes down to a single question: how much do you *really* want to succeed?

Onwards and upwards

- Studies tell us that people with more organizational savvy tend to do better in their careers. Consider that organizational savvy comprises four sub-skills: Social Astuteness (reading people's words and body language), Interpersonal Influence (changing minds), Networking Ability (building relationships with a range of people) and Demonstrable Sincerity (exhibiting visible integrity and honesty). Work out where you're weakest and think about the steps you could take to enhance your organizational savvy.

- Contemplate confiding in trusted friends who can advise you on how to hone your organizational savvy. The people who know us well may be able to help us to come up with better ideas than we could do on our own.

- If you're not sure how to boost your Interpersonal Influence skills, take a look back at Chapter 2: Winning the Argument. A lot of that earlier chapter was about building relationships, empathizing more effectively with people and finding ways to win them over to our ways of thinking.

- People who understand their strengths and weaknesses tend to be more effective than those who seek to do everything. Think about the different types of strengths and weaknesses that you have. Remember that being good (or bad) at something is different from enjoying (or not enjoying) it.

- Once you've identified your strengths and shortcomings, think about ways of changing the nature of your work so that you can exercise more of your Realized Strengths and Unrealized Strengths and fewer of your Genuine Weaknesses.

- Remember that developing your organizational savvy and playing more to your strengths are not mutually exclusive activities. If you want to win the race, you can work on both at the same time.

Conclusions

Onwards, Upwards and Over to You

It takes as much energy to wish as it does to plan.
Eleanor Roosevelt

This book is titled *How To Win*. It's about developing a winning outlook. It's about winning arguments by influencing and persuading people. It's about delivering winning pitches that engross and convince people. It's about winning the job by reaching out to people and delivering an outstanding interview performance. And it's about winning the career race by developing your organizational savvy and applying your strengths.

Those are all the ways in which we can win. But allow me for a few moments to tell you about two guaranteed ways to *lose*.

Lose by doing nothing

Of course, one sure-fire way to lose in your career is to do nothing. Simply finish reading the book, put it aside and get on with your day-to-day job. Because some people may finish this book and think that they now *understand* what it takes to succeed. But understanding is not the same as *doing*.

A couple of years ago an acquaintance I'll call Sheena told me that she was miserable in her work as an executive at a publishing company. A somewhat flighty individual with an up-and-down temperament, she wanted to enhance her career prospects and asked me to recommend a book I'd written that could help her out.

She ended up reading *E is for Exceptional: The New Science of Success* (Pan Books), which I wrote a few years ago. She told me that she sped through it and loved it. She said that it gave her a lot to think about and that she would try to apply some of the lessons when she was less busy at work. Maybe she would have time in a few weeks after a particularly busy period.

But the weeks turned into months and the months stretched on and on. She never did get the chance to do anything about what she had learnt from the book – or, more correctly, she never made it a priority. She never blocked out the time to devise a plan of action for how she would escape her unhappy situation.

Fast forward nearly three years to the present and she's still stuck in the same job. She has seen a couple of teammates overtake her; she has talked in envy about her colleagues who left the company to go on to bigger and better things. But she still grumbles about how no one takes her seriously enough and how much she wants to get out. A colleague said that she is one of those weird people who almost seem to prefer moaning about their lot in life rather than doing something to improve it.

The point? Reading this book and understanding the principles is not enough. It's application – doing and action – that gets results.

It's the people who complete the written exercises, refer back to the chapters of this book and make a plan that get the benefits. It's the individuals who apply the skills, maybe make a few missteps, but learn, improve and grow in both skill and confidence that get the uptick in their performance. It's those who talk to friends and confidants about how they can tweak their jobs that get the recognition and rewards.

Do and you win. Put this book aside and you lose.

Reading this book and understanding the principles is not enough. It's application – doing and action – that gets results.

Lose by doing too much

With so much content in this book, you'd be forgiven for wanting to tackle everything at once. But there's another way to lose. And that's by doing *too much*.

In this book we have covered many concepts. We began with the growth versus gifts mind-sets. In terms of winning arguments, we discussed more than a half-dozen tips and techniques for improving our abilities to pre-empt quarrels and coax people to see things our way.

When it comes to delivering winning pitches, I suggested the "SOAR vividly" method for telling effective, engaging stories. But there were other principles too: turning molehills back into mountains and checking that our stories transport people away, to name just two.

Jumping ahead to the chapter on winning the race, we encountered the concept of organizational savvy and its four distinct sub-skills. Plus we discussed the importance of identifying and applying our four types of strengths and weaknesses.

The point is that this book is stuffed to bursting with content. There are nearly two dozen diverse concepts and techniques for revamping your life. And anyone who tries to tackle everything – or even half of what's in this book – at once is almost certainly doomed to failure.

When I work with clients, we typically work on no more than a handful of issues at once. One current client is working on her networking and relationship-building skills. Another client I'm working with at the moment is singly focused on improving his presentation skills by telling better stories and doing so more charismatically. A third client is looking for a job in IT sales so we're working on his interview patter. What they all have in common is that each of them is working on just a couple of things at once.

While it's, of course, admirable to want to improve yourself, be careful not to attempt too much at once. Better to focus on a handful of tasks or actions and get to do them well before you move on to a new bunch of activities. Otherwise, it would be like trying to learn Italian, take tennis lessons, write a novel, lose weight and take up kung fu *all at the same time.*

Be careful not to attempt too much at once.

Plan, Do, Review

When I work with clients, I encourage them to work through what I call the "Plan, Do, Review loop". I suggest to clients that that they:

- Plan what they intend to do by writing out a plan of action.

- Do what they committed to do in their plan.

- Afterwards, review what they did, how it went and how they can do better on the next cycle. Then it's back to writing out a new plan.

Plan   Do

Review

The Plan, Do, Review loop is based on decades of research telling us that people who *write down* plans about what they intend to do are significantly more likely to follow through and actually overhaul their lives than people who simply have good intentions and think about what they want to do *in their heads*.

In study after study, researchers have found that people all over the world who *write down* their plans are more successful at changing their lives in all manner of ways. Fact: people are more likely to eat healthily and lose weight when they *write down* their plans. Fact: individuals wanting to quit smoking or excessive drinking are more successful when they *write down* what they will do and when.

Even students are more likely to complete their assignments when they *write down* their commitments. And managers are more successful at picking up new skills in the workplace when they – you guessed it – *write down* their plans.[1]

Taking the time to write down (or type up) plans is not optional. If you only take one thing away from this entire book, I would argue that it would be this.

Plan, Do, Review: Step 1 – *Plan*

Begin by figuring out what would make the biggest difference to your career. Flicking back through the chapters of this book, what activities or changes do you feel would give you the biggest boost at work?

There may be quite a few things you'd *like* to work on. But what are the most critical handful, the ones that would contribute most significantly to your career satisfaction and success?

Next, think about how you will actually carry each of them out. Think about *what* you will do, *how* exactly you will do it, *who* you could involve and *when* you will do it.

I've found the following table useful in my work with clients. There are four columns for the actions an individual can take. And then there's a final space at the bottom for a client to fill out the thing they'll do first. Here's what a blank table looks like:

What will I do?	*How* exactly will I do it?	*Who* could be involved?	*When* will I do it?

And what I will do *first* is to. . .

Clients usually find it useful to fill out a separate table for *each* different skill area that they want to work on. For example, suppose that a taciturn woman called Mei Li decides that she wants to work on her organizational savvy and assertiveness skills. That's two distinct skills, requiring two action plans.

Let's look at one of these plans, the one she puts together for tackling her assertiveness. Having worked through the questionnaire in Chapter 2: Winning the Argument, she writes out her plan as follows:

What will I do?	*How* exactly will I do it?	*Who* could be involved?	*When* will I do it?
Remind myself of the need to be assertive	Re-read Chapter 2 on arguments	—	Next month on 31st July
Prepare for meetings	Before big, diarized meetings, spend 10 minutes writing bullet points about what I want to say	Talk to Padmal before weekly team meetings for input. Email Joanna for updates before departmental meetings	Before weekly team meetings, quarterly finance meetings and departmental committee meetings

(Continued)

What will I do?	*How* exactly will I do it?	*Who* could be involved?	*When* will I do it?
Listen and empathize with Norman	Rather than beginning our conversations with what I want, begin by asking him how he feels about the issue and then let him rant	—	When I have my monthly telephone call with him
Use the DEAR method	Re-read the section on the DEAR method and write notes on what I want to say	Ask Alice for help – maybe to role play with me so I can practise first?	When making requests to Peter or Evelina, e.g. asking Peter for more budget next Wednesday
Prepare rigorously for my performance appraisal	Prepare arguments (using DEAR method)	—	Start working on this 1st October so I'm ready for November

And what I will do *first* is to . . . Email Alice today offering to buy her lunch to show her this action plan and get her advice on how to make all of this come off successfully

The idea of having a separate section at the bottom of the table for "And what I will do *first* is to . . ." is to get started. Some people put things off because they're lacking in confidence or feeling tired or lazy. But your life won't get better – you won't get the recognition, the promotion, the career contentment and rewards – from waiting. So this space is designed for something that you can do quickly today.

Some people reading this may think, "I'll do this later". But the readers who actually *write down* their plans are the ones who are most likely to succeed.

> ## Writing out your own action plan
>
> Having good intentions is not enough. Psychological research tells us very clearly that people who turn their intentions into action plans (or to use the psychological jargon "implementation intention plans") are significantly more likely to achieve their goals.
>
> When I coach clients in a typical 90-minute session, we always spend the last 10 to 15 minutes working out what they are promising to do, who they could involve and when they will do it. Will you do the same?

Plan, Do, Review: Step 2 – *Do*

The next step in the Plan, Do, Review loop is to actually *do* what you set out in your plan.

There's a famous quote from Benjamin Franklin that I like: "You may delay, but time will not." For me it's a great reminder that time ticks by. Put off what we know we could be doing and the weeks could so easily turn into months and the months into years.

If you want more help in not only putting together your action plan but also acting upon it, you could pick up one of my other books.

You Can Change Your Life: Easy Steps to Getting What You Want (Macmillan) contains advice on boosting your willpower, deploying visualization techniques to strengthen your resolve and enlisting the support of friends and colleagues to give you the best shot at improving yourself and, ultimately, changing your life.

Plan, Do, Review: Step 3 – *Review*

The final step in the Plan, Do, Review loop is to review what you did and how it went. So set aside a little time to think about your progress. In my experience, this consists of asking yourself three main questions:

- **"What worked well?"** Looking back at what you did and the results you got, what were you pleased with? What should you continue to do?

- **"What could I do better or differently next time?"** What could have worked better?

- **"How appropriate are my remaining plans?"** Looking forward to what you have yet to do in your action plan, is there anything that you may need to alter?

Just as crucial as the questions you ask yourself is the way you frame your own responses. You'll remember in Chapter 1: Developing a Winning Outlook, we discussed the difference between the growth versus gifts mind-sets. People with the gifts mind-set look at missteps and failures as signs to give up because they're not talented or gifted enough. But people with the growth outlook see even catastrophes and disasters as mere opportunities to continue learning. For a handy summary of the differences between the two attitudes on life, you could flick back to the section "Growing your confidence and capabilities" in Chapter 1 and in particular the table on page 29.

Understanding how best to review and plan your progress

Are you more of an introvert or an extravert?

When it comes to reviewing your progress and re-planning your next steps, are you the kind of person who likes to reflect quietly and work on your own? Or do you prefer to talk things through with other people?

Or maybe you like a combination of the two. Perhaps you like to work on some issues by yourself but would value the advice of trusted friends or colleagues to discuss weightier problems or larger opportunities.

Plan, Do, Review isn't something that you have to do alone. By all means make plans and review them privately if that's your style. Or talk about your plans with a confidant or a loved one. Do whatever works for you.

Oh, and if you'd like to delve further into your level of introversion/extraversion (as well as several other dimensions of personality), you could take a look at my book *Personality: How to Unleash Your Hidden Strengths* (Prentice Hall Life).

The science of effective reviews

When it comes to developing your skills – anything from improving your culinary prowess to getting better at a sport – how do you keep track of your progress? Are you someone who celebrates your successes, the milestones you've passed along the way? Or do you keep your eyes firmly on your goals and what you have yet to achieve?

You may be wondering why it matters. But to explain, I'll share one final research study which will allow you to make faster progress towards your goals.

A team of scientists led by Florida State University psychologist Kyle Conlon advertised online to recruit men and women who wanted to lose weight. Over a hundred participants attended an initial meeting in which they were given advice on how to lose weight; they also set goals as to how much weight they would ideally but safely be able to lose. Over the course of 12 weeks, the scientists monitored how much weight each individual actually lost.

Without their knowledge, the participants were randomly split into two groups. During weekly review meetings, the first group were told to focus on how much progress they had made (i.e. how much weight they shed each week). The second group were told to focus on their goals (i.e. how much weight they *still* needed to lose in order to hit their targets).

One group lost more than twice as much body fat as the other group.[2] But which would *you* guess would be more motivating? To focus on what you have accomplished or to focus on your goals?

Some commentators argue that it's a good idea to celebrate your achievements and congratulate yourself every time you make progress. However, the results of the study tell us that it was the participants who focused on what they had *yet* to achieve who lost the most weight. Remember that they lost *more than twice* as much body fat as those who focused on what they had already achieved.

In other words, focusing on our past accomplishments – on how far we've come – may end up reducing our enthusiasm. Perhaps looking back gives us a false sense of security. We risk resting on our laurels and coasting.

In contrast, focusing on our goals – on how far we still have to go – may help us to feel more inspired and motivated. Ultimately, *looking forward helps us to achieve better results*. Rather than allowing ourselves to be satisfied with the steps we've taken, we set our jaws and resolve to push on even further.

> Focusing on our goals – on how far we still have to go – may help us to feel more inspired and motivated.

Reviewing your progress

University researcher Kyle Conlon and his colleagues suggest that we can keep our motivation high by keeping our "eyes on the prize". One way of doing this is to compare ourselves to the role models we aspire to be like rather than the people we've overtaken.

For example, say you get a promotion. Rather than thinking how much better off you are than the colleagues languishing on the rungs below you, you could focus on what you need to do to reach the next step.

Or imagine you're a charity worker on a mission to feed starving people in a developing country. You could sit back by thinking, "I've helped thousands of people to have disease-free, healthy lives." Or you could spur yourself on by reminding yourself that "I've still got tens of thousands of people to help."

Then glance at your action plan to see what else you have yet to achieve. Which of your existing actions may need course-correcting? Or what entirely new actions may you need to add into your action plan? That way, you keep the momentum going rather than risk resting on your laurels.

Plan, Do, Review – and do it all over again

I know of a particularly highflying executive called Vaughn who uses the Plan, Do, Review method daily. The chief operating officer at a burgeoning Internet business, he begins each week on a Sunday evening at home by taking a few minutes to plan the major tasks he wishes to work on the next day. Most of those are to do with his work, but some aren't – he plays in a five-a-side football league and strives to get home early enough to have dinner with his wife and young children on certain nights of the week too.

When he arrives at work on Monday, he fights diligently to complete his priorities. One example: he schedules regular one-to-one meetings with each member of his team aimed at building their confidence and capability so that they too can manage their own teams as the business continues to grow.

Some days Vaughn gets nearly everything on his plan done. Other days he has to be flexible when issues spring up, such as system crashes, investor requests or unexpected client opportunities. But by having a plan, he can make better trade-offs in his decision-making about how to spend his time rather than constantly reacting to what everyone else wants of him.

At the end of each day, he reviews how things went. Should the systems problem that cropped up really have warranted his attention – or should he have left it to one of his team, for example? How could he pre-empt that client complaint next time? Did he spend too much time – or not enough – on internal meetings? And then he plans the next day.

But Vaughn's planning cycle doesn't just encompass what happened over the last day. Every year in August when his work is quietest, he takes an afternoon to review his progress over the past year before planning for the next. Is his work still fulfilling? But, at the same time, is he making the most of his life outside of work?

Looking forward, can he see himself in the same business in 12 months' time? What skills does he need to pick up to stay at the forefront of his field? What adventures or activities would he like to experience for the hell of it? Which relationships does he want to invest in further – and how?

Looking further ahead

What are your medium- to long-term goals? Where would you like to be in, say, 6 to 12 months' time?

Plans don't have to be followed slavishly. The point of a plan – whether a quick daily Plan, Do, Review plan or a more in-depth annual one – isn't to do everything on it irrespective of what else may be happening in your life. But it gives you a focus. It helps you to identify what's important rather than allowing yourself to be buffeted by everything else going on around you.

Of course, you're welcome to review and plan using whatever questions you like. But here are some prompts:

- Looking back on the last year, what have you learnt?
- What would you like to be different in the future?
- What steps will you take to achieve the changes you desire?

Putting it all into practice

Planning what you would like to do, doing it and reviewing how you got on isn't rocket science. In fact, I often say to clients that change needn't be hard. The theory is simple. It just takes diligent practice and persistent application to get the results.

Think about it this way: consider the theory versus practice of running a marathon. We all understand the theory behind running a marathon. You put your running shoes on and run 26 miles. Easy.

But, of course, you actually need to train. You need to run and run and run. For day after day, week after week and month after month. At first you may only be able to run a mile or so. Your muscles may cramp up and your feet may get sore.

But after a few weeks, you may be able to run several miles. And you continue to run, run, run.

And then one momentous day you realize that you ran 10 miles. Wow. And then you run 12 and maybe 16 or 18 miles. Then 26 miles doesn't seem such a big deal.

The point I'm trying to make is that understanding the theory is very different from putting it into practice. Just like running a marathon, the theory behind success at work often isn't that difficult. The principles we covered in the chapters of this book may not have been all that surprising. But it's the people who put those rules and ideas into practice that win.

A final thought

To finish, I would like to share with you one of my all-time favourite quotes. The author Mark Twain once said: "Don't go around saying the world owes you a living; the world owes you nothing; it was here first."

I think the same can be said in so many areas of our lives. We could think about our careers and say: "Don't go around saying your organization owes you a living; the organization owes you nothing; it was here first." The same goes for your boss. Your boss owes you nothing.

The same may be true in our personal lives too. Expecting that our parents, husbands, wives or loved ones owe us something – that they *should* be the way we want them to be – is likewise an easy route to heartache.

It's a useful lesson in life to accept that *we* – and *not* our organizations, bosses or loved ones – have the responsibility for our careers, livelihoods and happiness. If we want that assignment, funding, pay rise, promotion or corner office, we have to take the steps to get it. If we want to feel fulfilled, happy or loved, we can do something about it. Simply waiting and hoping isn't a strategy.

> We – and not our organizations, bosses or loved ones – have the responsibility for our careers, livelihoods and happiness.

If you want to be a winner, you can. Choose to *do*, to take action, to work towards what you want. Go on. Do it. And you may just achieve it.

Onwards and upwards

- If you want to hone your skills, improve your performance at work and your satisfaction with life, *you can*. Make the effort to apply the ideas and techniques within this book and you will get the results. Think that you *understand* the concepts and techniques but do nothing and you will stay the same.

- Also bear in mind that taking on *too much* can be as bad as doing nothing. Successful individuals plan and prioritize what they want to do. We all only have 24 hours in the day. So begin with the handful of things that will make the biggest difference to your life and career. You can work on the rest later.

- Use the Plan, Do, Review method to work out how *exactly* you will achieve your goals. You may be able to complete some of your actions in days or weeks. Others may take months. But by continually reviewing what worked or didn't and re-planning, you can make sure that you make progress.

- Keep this book with you over the months and years. I hope that you will refer to it time and again in your quest to win the argument, the pitch, the job and the race.

- Let me know what you thought about this book. And tell me how you get on. You can message me on Twitter – I'm @ robyeung – feel free to say hello!

Notes

Chapter 1

1. One of the leading researchers in the field of how our attitudes can affect our progress in life is Stanford University professor Carol Dweck. For a primer on the differences between the gifts and growth mind-sets, see: Dweck, C. S. & Leggett, E. L. (1988). A social-cognitive approach to motivation and personality. *Psychological Review*, 95, 256–273.
2. Pollack, J. M., Burnette, J. L. & Hoyt, C. L. (2012). Self-efficacy in the face of threats to entrepreneurial success: Mind-sets matter. *Basic and Applied Social Psychology*, 34, 287–294.
3. Heslin, P. A., Vandewalle, D. & Latham, G. P. (2006). Keen to help? Managers' implicit person theories and their subsequent employee coaching. *Personnel Psychology*, 59, 871–902.
4. Blackwell, L., Trzesniewski, K. & Dweck, C. S. (2007). Implicit theories of intelligence predict achievement across an adolescent transition: A longitudinal study and an intervention. *Child Development*, 78, 246–263.
5. Burnette, J. L. (2010). Implicit theories of body weight: Entity beliefs can weigh you down. *Personality and Social Psychology Bulletin*, 36, 410–422.
6. Valentiner, D. P., Mounts, N. S., Durik, A. M. & Gier-Lonsway, S. L. (2011). Shyness mindset: Applying mindset theory to the domain of inhibited social behavior. *Personality and Individual Differences*, 50, 1174–1179.
7. O'Connor, A. J., Nemeth, C. J. & Akutsu, S. (2013). Consequences of beliefs about the malleability of creativity. *Creativity Research Journal*, 25, 155–162, http://www.tandfonline.com/doi/abs/10.1080/10400419 .2013.783739#.UiDklj_y0mg.

8. Scollon, C. N. & Diener, E. (2006). Love, work and changes in extraversion and neuroticism over time. *Journal of Personality and Social Psychology*, 91, 1152–1165.

9. Yeung, R. (2012). *E is for Exceptional: The New Science of Success.* London: Pan Books.

10. Some of these recommendations are adapted from a 2012 paper by a team of top psychologists from four leading universities: Burnette, J. L., O'Boyle, E. H., VanEpps, E. M., Pollack, J. M. & Finkel, E. J. (2012). Mind-sets matter: A meta-analytic review of implicit theories and self-regulation. *Psychological Bulletin*, 139, 655–701.

Chapter 2

1. Williams, E. R. & Akridge, R. L. (1996). The Responsible Assertion Scale: Development and evaluation of psychometric qualities. *Vocational Evaluation and Work Adjustment Bulletin*, 29, 19–23.

2. Ames, D. R. & Flynn, F. J. (2007). What breaks a leader: The curvilinear relation between assertiveness and leadership. *Journal of Personality and Social Psychology*, 92, 307–324.

3. Schill, T., Toves, C. & Ramanaiah, N. (1981). Responsible assertion and coping with stress. *Psychological Reports*, 49, 557–558.

4. For a review of the literature, see: Heimberg, R. G., Montgomery, D., Madsen Jr., C. H. & Heimberg, J. S. (1977). Assertion training: A review of the literature. *Behavior Therapy*, 8, 953–971.

5. Schwartz, R. M. & Gottman, J. (1976). Toward a task analysis of assertive behavior. *Journal of Consulting and Clinical Psychology*, 44, 910–920.

6. Kray, L. J., Galinsky, A. D. & Markman, K. D. (2009). Counterfactual structure and learning from experience in negotiations. *Journal of Experimental Social Psychology*, 45, 979–982.

7. Bruneau, E. G. & Saxe, R. (2012). The power of being heard: The benefits of "perspective-giving" in the context of intergroup conflict. *Journal of Experimental Social Psychology*, 48, 855–866.

8. Ancona, D., Malone, T. W., Orlinkowski, W. J. & Senge, P. M. (2007). In praise of the incomplete leader. *Harvard Business Review*, 85, 92–100.

9. Kleven, H. J., Knudsen, M. B., Kreiner, C. T., Pedersen, S. & Saez, E. (2011). Unwilling or unable to cheat? Evidence from a tax audit experiment in Denmark. *Econometrica*, 79, 651–692.

10. Halevy, N., Chou, E. Y. & Murnighan, J. K. (2012). Mind games: The mental representation of conflict. *Journal of Personality and Social Psychology*, 102, 132–148.

11. Fernald, A. & Mazzie, C. (1991). Prosody and focus in speech to infants and adults. *Developmental Psychology*, 27, 209–221.

12. Curhan, J. R. & Pentland, A. (2007). Thin slices of negotiation: Predicting outcomes from conversational dynamics within the first 5 minutes. *Journal of Applied Psychology*, 92, 802–811.

Chapter 3

1. For a recent overview of evolutionary psychological theories and how humans may be hardwired to tell and listen to stories, see: Saad, G. (2013). Evolutionary consumption. *Journal of Consumer Psychology*, 23, 351–371.

2. de Wit, J. B. F., Das, E. & Vet, R. (2008). What works best: Objective statistics or a personal testimonial? An assessment of the persuasive effects of different types of message evidence on risk perception. *Health Psychology*, 27, 110–115.

3. Wilson, T. D. & Brekke, N. (1994). Mental contamination and mental correction: Unwanted influences on judgments and evaluations. *Psychological Bulletin*, 116, 117–142.

4. Green, M. C. & Brock, T. C. (2000). The role of transportation in the persuasive of public narratives. *Journal of Personality and Social Psychology*, 79, 701–721.

5. If you want to watch the YouTube trailer for the American Red Cross campaign, visit: http://youtu.be/3yufZP-LZrk.

6. Small, D. A., Loewenstein, G. & Slovic, P. (2007). Sympathy and callousness: The impact of deliberative thought on donations to identifiable and statistical victims. *Organizational Behavior and Human Decision Processes*, 102, 143–153.

7. Kaufman, G. K. & Libby, L. K. (2012). Changing beliefs and behavior through experience-taking. *Journal of Personality and Social Psychology*, 103, 1–19.

Chapter 4

1. If you would like to read the original papers by the researcher Albert Mehrabian, you can take a look at: Mehrabian, A. & Wiener, M. (1967). Decoding of inconsistent communications. *Journal of Personality and Social Psychology*, 6, 109–114. Mehrabian, A. & Ferris, S. R. (1967). Inference of attitudes from nonverbal communication in two channels. *Journal of Consulting Psychology*, 31, 248–252.
2. Hollandsworth Jr., J. G., Kazelskis, R., Stevens, J. & Dressel, M. E. (1979). Relative contributions of verbal, articulative, and nonverbal communication to employment decisions in the job interview setting. *Personnel Psychology*, 32, 359–367.
3. Bartram, D. (2005). The great eight competencies: A criterion-centric approach to validation. *Journal of Applied Psychology*, 990, 1185–1203.
4. Yeung, R. (2011). *Successful Interviewing and Recruitment*. London: Kogan Page.
5. Harris, K. J. & Kacmar, K. M. (2007). The impact of political skill on impression management effectiveness. *Journal of Applied Psychology*, 92, 278–285.
6. Swider, B. W., Barrick, M. R., Harris, B. & Stoverink, A. C. (2011). Managing and creating an image in the interview: The role of interviewee initial impressions. *Journal of Applied Psychology*, 96, 1275–1288.
7. Quizzes B and C are adapted from a much more extensive measure of candidate behaviours by researchers Julia Levashina at Indiana University Kokomo and Michael Campion at Purdue University: Levashina, J. & Campion, M. A. (2007). Measuring faking in the employment interview: Development and validation of an interview faking behavior scale. *Journal of Applied Psychology*, 92, 1638–1656.

8. Higgins, C. A. & Judge, T. A. (2004). The effect of applicant influence tactics on recruiter perceptions of fit and hiring recommendations: A field study. *Journal of Applied Psychology*, 89, 622–632.

9. Barrick, M. R., Shaffer, J. A. & DeGrassi, S. W. (2009). What you see may not be what you get: Relationships among self-presentation tactics and ratings of interview and job performance. *Journal of Applied Psychology*, 94, 1394–1411.

10. Chaplin, W. F., Phillips, J. B., Brown, J. D., Clanton, N. R. & Stein, J. L. (2000). Handshaking, gender, personality and first impressions. *Journal of Personality and Social Psychology*, 79, 110–117.

11. Rasmussen, K. G. (1984). Nonverbal behavior, verbal behavior, résumé credentials, and selection interview outcomes. *Journal of Applied Psychology*, 69, 551–556.

12. Forbes, R. J. & Jackson, P. R. (1980). Non-verbal behaviour and the outcome of selection interviews. *Journal of Occupational Psychology*, 53, 65–72.

13. Barrick, M. R., Dustin, S. L., Giluk, T. L., Stewart, G. L., Shaffer, J. A. & Swider, B. W. (2011). Candidate characteristics driving initial impressions during rapport building: Implications for employment interview validity. *Journal of Occupational and Organizational Psychology*, 96, 1275–1288.

14. Pellizzari, M. (2010). Do friends and relatives really help in getting a good job? *Industrial and Labor Relations Review*, 63, 494–510.

15. Van Hoye, G., van Hooft, E. A. J. & Lievens, F. (2009). Networking as a job search behaviour: A social network perspective. *Journal of Occupational and Organizational Psychology*, 82, 661–682.

16. Forret, M. L. & Sullivan, S. E. (2002). A balanced scorecard approach to networking: A guide to successfully navigating career changes. *Organizational Dynamics*, 31, 245–258.

17. Thorsteinson, T. J. (2011). Initiating salary discussions with an extreme request: Anchoring effects on initial salary offers. *Journal of Applied Social Psychology*, 41, 1774–1792.

18. For a different example of anchoring, this time used to sell cans of soup in a supermarket, see: Wansink, B., Kent, R. J. & Hoch, S. J. (1998). An anchoring and adjustment model of purchase quantity decisions. *Journal of Marketing Research*, 35, 71–81.

19. Other research has found that humour elicits greater concessions from the people we're negotiating with too: O'Quin, K. & Aronoff,

J. (1981). Humor as a technique of social influence. *Social Psychology Quarterly*, 44, 349–357.

Chapter 5

1. Ferris, G. R., Treadway, D. C., Kolodinsky, R. W., Hochwarter, W. A., Kacmar, C. J., Douglas, C. & Frink, D. D. (2005). Development and validation of the political skill inventory. *Journal of Management*, 31, 126–152.
2. Semadar, A., Robins, G. & Ferris, G. R. (2006). Comparing the validity of multiple social effectiveness constructs in the prediction of managerial performance. *Journal of Organizational Behaviour*, 27, 443–461.
3. Meurs J. A., Coleman Gallagher, V. & Perrewé, P. L. (2010). The role of political skill in the stressor–outcome relationship: Differential predictions for self- and other-reports of political skill. *Journal of Vocational Behavior*, 76, 520–533.
4. Shi, J., Johnson, R. E., Liu, Y. & Wang, M. (2013). Linking subordinate political skill to supervisor dependence and reward recommendations. *Journal of Applied Psychology*, 98, 374–384.
5. For a recent review of research studies on organizational savvy, see: Bing, M. N., Davison, H. K., Minor, I., Novicevic, M. M. & Frink, D. D. (2011). The prediction of task and contextual performance by political skill: A meta-analysis and moderator test. *Journal of Vocational Behavior*, 79, 563–577.
6. One study tested people's organizational savvy and their intelligence and found no link. In other words, book smart so-called intelligent people could sometimes be poor at organizational savvy while less well-educated people could often be very good at organizational savvy. See: Ferris *et al.* (2005) note 1.
7. Waterman, A. S., Schwartz, S. J., Goldbacher, E., Green, H., Miller, C. & Philip, S. (2003). Predicting the subjective experience of intrinsic motivation: The roles of self-determination, the balance of challenges and skills, and self-realization values. *Personality and Social Psychology Bulletin*, 29, 1447–1458.

8. Peterson, C. & Seligman, M. E. P. (2004). *Character Strengths and Virtues: A Handbook and Classification*. Washington, DC: American Psychological Association.
9. Clifton, D. O. & Anderson, E. C. (2001–2002). *StrengthsQuest*. Washington, DC: Gallup Organization.
10. Gladwell, M. (2008). *Outliers: The Story of Success*. New York: Little, Brown & Company.
11. Hambrick, D. Z., Oswald, F. L., Altmann, E., Meinz, E. J., Gobet, F. & Campitelli, G. (in press). Deliberate practice: Is that all it takes to become an expert? *Intelligence*, http://dx.doi.org/10.1016/j.intell .2013.04.001.
12. Linley, A., Willars, J. & Biswas-Diener, R. (2010). *The Strengths Book*. Coventry: CAPP Press.

Conclusions

1. For a review of the research on planning and behaviour change, see: Gollwitzer, P. M. & Sheeran, P. (2006). Implementation intentions and goal achievement: A meta-analysis of effects and processes. *Advances in Experimental Social Psychology*, 38, 69–119.
2. Conlon, K. E., Ehrlinger, J., Eibach, R. P., Crescioni, A. W., Alquist, J. L., Gerend, M. A. & Dutton, G. R. (2011). Eyes on the prize: The longitudinal benefits of goal focus on progress toward a weight loss goal. *Journal of Experimental Social Psychology*, 47, 853–855.

Index